THE DESSERTS COOKBOOK

THE DESSERTS COOKBOOK

Elizabeth Pomeroy

OCTOPUS

Contents

This edition first published in 1978 by
Octopus Books Limited
59 Grosvenor Street, London W1

© 1977 Hennerwood Publications Limited

ISBN 0 7064 0769 5

Produced by Mandarin Publishers Limited,
22a Westlands Road, Quarry Bay, Hong Kong

Printed in Hong Kong

Introduction

One of the many delightful things about desserts is that there is always one to meet any occasion – grand or homely; any weather – midwinter or midsummer; any person – hearty eater or choosy gourmet; any budget – large or small.

The British are renowned for the variety of their hot, hearty puddings, the French for gâteaux and rich pastries, the Italians for ice creams and fresh fruit desserts. Which to choose?

First you have to consider whether it is to be a substantial part of the meal or a delicate finish.

If you are cooking for a family with the robust appetites of the energetic young, or adults engaged in strenuous work, one of the famous English hot puddings will be eaten with gusto and be both satisfying and inexpensive.

If you are having a party and the menu includes a rich main course, you need a light refreshing dessert to follow it – like Lemon Soufflé or Melon Sherbet. Alternatively you can plan the menu, say for a birthday, so that it builds up to the last course with a spectacular "greedy" dessert such as Gâteau St Honoré or a splendid Baba, gleaming with Rum Syrup and filled with whipped cream and strawberries. Some glamorous desserts which look

difficult are actually quite easy to make, like a Pavlova from Australia.

Puddings and custards are clearly making a come-back for a variety of reasons, not least economic, and not only give pleasure to family and friends but also provide fun and interest for the home cook. A mistaken idea about hot puddings is that they take too much time to make. In fact most of them are quick and easy to prepare and, once in the steamer, simmer away using very little heat and leaving one free for the next two or three hours to do other things. If you want to go out to shop, you can put the pudding in a deep pan or casserole in a low oven and it will look after itself. Another advantage in some families is that steamed puddings do not spoil if kept for late-comers.

For kitchen-dining room meals, there are delightful fried and pan-to-table desserts ranging from Poor Knights of Windsor (one of the happier ways of using up surplus bread) or delicious little honeyed Greek Fritters, to the exciting rum-flamed Pineapple Pancakes from the Caribbean.

If you find yourself with an unexpected guest and want a last-minute sweet, you will find a selection under "Quickies".

All spoon measurements are level.
All recipes serve four unless otherwise stated.

Suet crust pastry

1¾ cups self-rising flour
¼ teaspoon salt
⅔ cup shredded suet
Cold water to mix

Sift the flour and salt together and rub in the suet lightly with the fingertips. Add just sufficient water to mix to a soft but not sticky dough, using a knife and your fingers. Turn onto a floured board and pat into a smooth ball. Use as required.

Variation
If preferred 1¾ cups all-purpose flour with 2 teaspoons baking powder may be used instead of self-rising flour. One-half cup of the flour may be replaced by ½ cup of fresh white bread-crumbs which will give a lighter and more spongy crust. This is sometimes liable to break if the pudding is turned out of the basin.

Note : Suet is beef fat – specifically, it is the fat from around the kidney area. It is dry and hard and therefore a little easier to work with than the oilier fat found around other muscles and organs. However, any beef fat will do, as long as it is fresh smelling and cleaned of any meat or membrane.
When shredding or chopping suet, dip the fat into flour frequently to keep the flakes separate and from sticking to the grater or knife. The more finely shredded or chopped, the lighter the pudding. Don't shred or chop until you are ready to use it. Shredded suet can be used as either the fat in a pie or pastry dough – see Suet Crust Pastry (above) – or combined with flour and/or breadcrumbs in pudding mixtures.
Traditionally puddings are made in pudding basins. These are pottery bowls made with a rim under which the pudding covering is secured. In place of a pudding basin, you can use a stainless steel or ovenproof glass bowl.

Blackberry and apple hat

Suet crust (see above)
3 medium cooking apples
1½ cups blackberries
2–3 tablespoons brown
or white sugar
Scant ½ cup cold water

Cooking Time: 3 hours

The combination of blackberry with apple is an old favorite, and never better than when inside a suet crust.
Grease a 5 cup pudding basin. Roll out the suet crust into a circle about ¼ inch thick. Cut out a quarter and line the basin (see opposite). Peel, core and slice the apples and fill the basin, layering the apples with blackberries and sugar. Gather the remaining suet crust into a ball and roll it out into a circle to put on top of the fruit. Damp the edge all round.
Trim the lining pastry neatly about ½ inch above the lid, fold the edges over and press onto the lid. Cover the basin and steam the pudding (see page 10) for 3 hours. Lift out and allow to shrink slightly. Place a hot serving platter on top, invert the platter and basin together and unmold carefully. Serve hot with a bowl of brown sugar and custard sauce or plain whipped cream.

Lining a bowl with suet crust pastry; Blackberry and apple hat

Variations

Fruit fillings
This traditional English pudding can be filled with any fresh fruit in season or with dried apricots, peaches or prunes which have been soaked overnight.

Pear and walnut pudding
Slice pears and chop walnuts, flavor with finely grated lemon rind or crushed coriander seeds and brown sugar.

Plum, apricot or greengage pudding
Halve and stone fruit and layer with sugar.

Gooseberry pudding
Top and tail gooseberries, layer with brown sugar spiced with grated nutmeg.

Rhubarb pudding
Cut rhubarb in 1 inch lengths, flavor with grated orange rind and juice or chopped ginger and white or brown sugar.

How to line a pudding basin with suet crust
1. Roll out suet crust thinly 4 inches larger all round than the top of the basin. Cut out a quarter.
2. Fold remaining pastry into three, place inside the greased basin and unfold carefully. Press pastry evenly all round basin, dampen cut edges and press firmly together.
3. Fill with prepared mixture. Gather remaining quarter into a ball, roll out into a circle to fit top of basin and place on top of filling.
4. Trim lining pastry about $\frac{1}{2}$ inch above lid, dampen edge, fold over onto lid and press together.

Four fruit layer pudding

Suet crust (see page 8)
1⅓ cups blackberries
¾ cup sugar
½ lb fresh apricots, halved and pitted
½ lb red or purple plums, halved and pitted
½ lb pears, sliced

Cooking Time: 2½–3 hours

You can use a selection of any fresh or dried fruit for this pudding, but it looks most attractive with layers of contrasting colors.

Grease a 5 cup pudding basin and prepare a steamer. Roll out suet crust thinly. Cut out a small circle to fit the bottom of the basin and come ½ inch up the side to form a cap. Spread with blackberries and sprinkle with sugar. Cut out a larger circle of pastry and cover fruit. Spread with apricots, cut side uppermost, and sprinkle with sugar. Cut out a larger circle of pastry and spread with plums and sugar. Cut out and cover with another circle of pastry. Spread with sliced pears and sugar and cover with remaining pastry to form a lid. Tie greased foil over basin and steam for 2½–3 hours. Remove from heat, allow to shrink and turn out onto a warm platter. Serve hot with plain whipped cream or Syrup Sauce (see page 14).

To cover a steamed pudding

Method 1 (traditional for suet puddings)
Lay a piece of buttered paper on top of the pudding. Cut a square of white cotton cloth 12 inches larger than the width of the pudding basin. Cover the pudding and make a 1 inch pleat across the center. Tie down securely with string and open pleat to allow mixture to rise underneath. Draw opposite corners of the square together and knot – this makes a convenient handle by which to lift the pudding in and out of the saucepan.

Method 2 (suitable for sponge puddings)
Take a bowl or metal pudding mold large enough to allow the mixture to rise during cooking. Cut a square of foil 6 inches larger than the width of the bowl and grease well. Cover the pudding with it, pleating the foil firmly down the sides of the bowl or tying it down with string.

Method 3
Use a plastic bowl with clip-on lid. Do not overfill with mixture – allow room for it to rise. Grease inside of lid before clipping on bowl. The pudding will take 20–30 minutes longer to cook in plastic than in oven-proof glass or pottery, or in a metal mold.

How to steam puddings

There are various ways to steam puddings, according to the equipment available. The most important thing is to make sure the pudding is properly covered and that the water is kept simmering, but never boils over the top of the pudding or boils away from underneath leaving the saucepan dry.

Method 1
Place pudding in a steamer over a saucepan of simmering water. Put lid on steamer and check periodically that water has not boiled away underneath. Puddings take longer to cook in a steamer than when immersed in water.

Method 2
Place pudding in a pan converter and using hooks or tongs lower into a saucepan which contains sufficient simmering water to come only half way up the pudding bowl. If no pan converter is available make a sling with a broad strip of double foil long enough to lift the pudding in and out of the saucepan. Put on pan lid and cook over gentle heat. Add more boiling water as required but make sure the water does not boil over the pudding.

Method 3
A pressure cooker is excellent for steaming puddings as it saves time and fuel. It is essential that the manufacturer's instructions are followed precisely.

Covering a pudding for steaming; Four fruit layer pudding

Baked roly-poly pudding

Suet crust (see page 8)
⅓ cup jam, warmed
Milk and sugar for glazing (optional)

Cooking Time: 30–40 minutes
Oven: 400°F

Roll out the suet crust about ¼ inch thick into a rectangle about 10 × 8 inches. Spread evenly with warm jam leaving a border about ½ inch wide all round. Fold this border over the jam and brush with water. Roll up, not too tightly, from one of the shorter sides. Press the top edge down, seal it and press the ends together.

Turn roly-poly upside down on a piece of greased foil or wax paper large enough to come halfway up the sides of the roll. Tie loosely about 2 inches from each end, leaving room for the pastry to rise. Cut 4 slits across pastry top to allow the steam to escape. Brush lightly with milk and sprinkle with sugar; alternatively dust with sugar after baking. Bake in a hot oven for 30–40 minutes until well risen and golden. Remove paper case and serve hot with plain whipped cream or custard sauce.

Variations

Steamed roly-poly

Cooking Time: 1½–2 hours

Prepare a saucepan of boiling water with steamer on top. Make the roly-poly as for baking, above. Turn it upside down on a sheet of greased foil large enough to wrap round it, leaving room for the pastry to rise. Seal the ends on top and sides by pleating or rolling them firmly together. Place in the steamer and cook for 1½–2 hours (see page 10). When cooked, open foil and roll pudding carefully onto a warm serving dish. Serve hot with custard sauce or Jam Sauce (see page 14).

Mincemeat and syrup roly-poly
Spread suet crust with mincemeat and trickle over 2–3 tablespoons golden or light corn syrup.

Baked apple dumplings

Suet crust (see page 8)
4 medium apples
4 heaped teaspoons brown sugar or mincemeat
1 egg white, beaten
4 teaspoons sugar

Cooking Time: 30 minutes
Oven 400°F

Roll out the suet crust thinly into a square and cut into four equal pieces. Peel and core the apples and put one in the center of each pastry square. Fill the apple center with brown sugar or mincemeat. Brush the edge of each pastry square with water, draw the corners up to meet over the center of each apple and press the edges firmly together. Decorate with pastry leaves. Put in a greased baking tin. Brush with egg white and sprinkle with sugar. Bake in a hot oven for 30 minutes. Serve hot with Rum Butter (see page 22).

Variation

Steamed apple dumplings
Prepare apples and wrap in suet crust as above. Place each dumpling upside down on a square of greased foil large enough to wrap loosely round it, allowing room for the pastry to rise. Place the dumplings in a steamer over a saucepan of boiling water and cook for 45–60 minutes. Serve hot with Apricot Jam Sauce (see page 14).

Baked roly-poly pudding; Baked apple dumplings

Steamed college pudding

⅓ cup self-rising flour
1 cup brown breadcrumbs
½ teaspoon ground allspice
2½ tablespoons brown sugar
⅓ cup shredded suet
¾ cup mixed dried fruit (dark raisins,
golden raisins, currants)
¼ cup candied peel, chopped
1 egg, beaten
3–4 tablespoons milk

Cooking Time: 2–2½ hours

Grease a 4 cup pudding basin and prepare a steamer. Mix together the dry ingredients. Mix in the beaten egg and enough milk to produce a soft consistency which drops easily from the spoon in 5 seconds. Turn into the basin, cover with greased foil and tie down securely. Steam for 2–2½ hours (see page 10). Remove from heat and allow to shrink slightly before turning out. Serve hot with Lemon Foam Sauce (see page 26) or Brandy Butter (see page 22).

Snowdon pudding

1 cup raisins
¼ cup glacé cherries, halved
⅔ cup shredded suet
2 cups breadcrumbs
3 tablespoons rice flour
Finely grated rind of 1 lemon
¼ cup lemon marmalade
2 eggs, beaten
3–4 tablespoons milk

Cooking Time: 1½–2 hours

This is a warming and satisfying Welsh pudding well suited to climbers or other hungry and energetic folk. Prepare a steamer and grease a 5 cup pudding mold. Decorate the mold with some of the raisins and the glacé cherries, cut side down. Mix together the rest of the raisins with the dry ingredients. Stir in the marmalade and eggs and add enough milk to make a soft dropping consistency. Spoon carefully into the pudding mold so as not to disarrange the cherries and raisins. Cover with greased foil and steam for 1½–2 hours (see page 10). Remove from heat and allow to shrink slightly before unmolding. Serve hot with Sherry Foam Sauce (see page 26).

Orange marmalade pudding

⅓ cup orange marmalade
¾ cup flour
Pinch of salt
1 teaspoon baking powder
1 cup breadcrumbs
⅔ cup shredded suet
Finely grated rind of 1 lemon
¼ cup sugar
2 eggs, beaten
⅔ cup milk

Cooking Time: 1½–2 hours

This is an easy pudding to make and you can vary it by using different marmalades – lemon, grapefruit, lime or ginger. Serve it with a matching Marmalade Sauce.
Grease a 4 cup pudding basin. Spread 1 tablespoon marmalade over the bottom. Prepare a steamer. Sift together the flour, salt and baking powder. Mix in the breadcrumbs, suet, lemon rind and sugar. Stir in remaining marmalade and eggs and sufficient milk to give a soft dropping consistency. Turn into the basin, cover with greased foil and tie down tightly. Steam (see page 10) for 1½–2 hours. Remove from steamer and allow to shrink slightly before turning out. Serve hot with Orange Marmalade Sauce.

Marmalade sauce

¼ cup marmalade
⅔ cup hot water
1 teaspoon cornstarch
2 tablespoons cold water
Lemon juice to taste

Heat marmalade and hot water in a small pan. Mix cornstarch to a smooth paste with the cold water. Remove pan from heat and blend in the cornstarch mixture. Boil for 3 minutes and sharpen to taste with lemon juice.

Variation

Jam or syrup sauce

Follow recipe for Marmalade Sauce substituting jam or 3 tablespoons golden or light corn syrup.

Steamed college pudding; Snowdon pudding; Orange marmalade pudding

Steamed cherry pudding

6 oz fresh cherries
1¼ cups breadcrumbs
3 tablespoons sugar
Finely grated rind of ½ lemon
1¼ cups light cream or evaporated milk
2 eggs, separated

For the cherry sauce:
¼ lb fresh cherries
⅔ cup water
3 tablespoons sugar
Juice of ½ lemon
2 teaspoons cornstarch
1 tablespoon Cherry Brandy or Kirsch (optional)

Cooking Time: 1½ hours

Remove stems and pits from cherries. (Cherries are easily pitted with a cherry pitter; alternatively, open one end of a paper clip and use this to hook them out.) Mix with the breadcrumbs, sugar and lemon rind. Heat cream or evaporated milk, bring to the boil and pour over the mixture.

Beat the egg whites until stiff, but not brittle. Beat the yolks with a fork and stir into the pudding mixture. Fold in the whites and turn into a well-buttered 2½ cup bowl or pudding mold. Cover with greased foil and steam (see page 10) for 1½ hours until well risen and firm to the touch. Meanwhile make the Cherry Sauce. Remove stems and pits from the cherries and put in a small saucepan with the water, sugar and lemon juice. Cover and simmer for 15 minutes. Mix the cornstarch to a thin paste with 2 tablespoons water and stir in 2 tablespoons of the cherry liquid. Blend this mixture back into the saucepan and simmer, stirring well, for 2 minutes. Remove from heat and add the Cherry Brandy or Kirsch if using.

When the pudding is cooked, allow to shrink slightly before unmolding onto a warm serving plate. Pour on the Cherry Sauce.

Rich chocolate pudding

3 oz semi-sweet chocolate
4 tablespoons butter or margarine
1¼ cups milk
5 tablespoons sugar
¼ teaspoon vanilla extract
2 eggs, separated
2½ cups fresh white breadcrumbs

Cooking Time: 1½–2 hours

Put the chocolate and butter in a bowl over a saucepan of hot water until melted. Remove from heat and stir until smooth. Warm the milk and add it gradually. Stir in the sugar. Add vanilla to the beaten egg yolks and stir into the chocolate. Mix in breadcrumbs. Beat the egg whites until stiff but not brittle and fold into the mixture. Turn into a well-greased 4 cup pudding mold. Cover closely with greased foil and steam (see page 10) for 1½–2 hours until well risen and springy to the touch. Allow to shrink before unmolding. Serve hot with Chocolate Sauce (see page 74) or cold with plain whipped cream.

Rich chocolate pudding; Steamed cherry pudding; Guards' pudding

Guards' pudding

3 cups fresh breadcrumbs
Scant ½ cup sugar
2 eggs, beaten
6 tablespoons melted butter
¼ cup raspberry jam
¼ teaspoon baking soda
1 teaspoon water

Cooking Time: 2 hours

Mix the breadcrumbs and sugar together well. Stir in the eggs, the melted butter and jam. Dissolve the baking soda in the water and stir thoroughly into the mixture. Turn into a well-greased 4 cup pudding mold. Cover with greased foil and steam (see page 10) for 2 hours until set. Allow to shrink before unmolding. Serve hot with custard sauce or plain whipped cream.

Queen of puddings

1½ cups fresh white breadcrumbs
2 tablespoons sugar
2 teaspoons finely grated lemon rind
2 tablespoons butter or margarine
2 cups milk
2 eggs, separated
2 tablespoons raspberry jam
¼ cup superfine sugar
Sugar for dusting

To decorate:
Glacé cherries
Angelica

Cooking Time: 1 hour
Oven: 325°F

Vary this old favorite by putting raspberries or blackberries in the bottom of the dish.

Mix together the breadcrumbs and 2 tablespoons sugar. Add the lemon rind and butter to the milk and heat gently until the butter melts, then pour over the breadcrumbs. Stir well and leave to swell for 30 minutes. Beat the egg yolks and blend into the cooled mixture. Pour into a well-greased 4 cup ovenproof dish. Bake in a preheated warm oven for 30 minutes or until firm and set. Warm the jam and spread over the pudding. Beat the egg whites until stiff and dry. Fold in the superfine sugar and pile on top of the pudding. Swirl or ruffle the top and dust with sugar. Decorate with glacé cherries and angelica. Return the pudding to the oven and bake for 30 minutes or until crisp and golden. Serve hot or cold.

Friar's omelette

3 large cooking apples (about 1½ lb)
Finely grated rind of 1 lemon
Pinch of ground cloves or cinnamon
¼–½ cup sugar
3 egg yolks, beaten
1½ cups breadcrumbs
6 tablespoons butter or margarine

Cooking Time: 1 hour
Oven: 375°F

Wipe and core the apples. Pour sufficient water into a roasting pan to cover the base thinly and put in the apples. Lay a sheet of well-buttered foil on top and bake in a moderately hot oven for 30 minutes or until tender; test with a skewer. Remove from oven and scrape out the pulp into a basin. Add the lemon rind, spice and sugar to taste. Beat in the egg yolks.

Butter a 4 cup pie dish or shallow casserole and spread a thick layer of breadcrumbs in the bottom. Pour over the apple mixture and cover with remaining crumbs. Dot all over with little knobs of butter or melt the butter and pour it over. Return to oven and bake for 30 minutes or until crisp and golden on top. Serve hot with plain whipped cream or custard sauce.

Bread and butter pudding

6 slices white bread
4–6 tablespoons butter
½ cup raisins or currants or a mixture of both
¼ cup sugar
2 large or 3 small eggs
2½ cups milk

Cooking Time: 45–60 minutes
Oven: 325°F

An agreeable way of using up surplus sliced bread is this quickly-made, ever-popular pudding.

Remove crusts from bread and spread thickly with butter. Cut each slice into four, either squares or triangles. Butter a 5 cup ovenproof dish, preferably rectangular. Arrange buttered bread over the bottom of the dish and sprinkle with fruit and sugar. Put in another layer of bread, the rest of the fruit and half the remaining sugar. Cover with remaining bread, butter side uppermost and sprinkle on the rest of the sugar. Beat the eggs well into the milk and pour over the pudding. Leave to stand for 30 minutes or so to allow the bread to absorb the milk. Bake in a warm oven for 45–60 minutes until set and the top is crisp and golden. Serve hot.

Friar's omelette; Bread and butter pudding; Queen of puddings

Summer pudding

2 lb mixed soft fruit
½–¾ cup sugar
About ½ a loaf of bread

Cooking Time: 15–20 minutes

Aptly named, Summer Pudding contains a medley of any soft summer fruits available: raspberries, blackberries, red or black-currants and cherries.

Pick over the fruit, removing stems and pits. This should leave 1½ lb of prepared fruit. Put the fruit and sugar in a thick pan over very gentle heat and stir carefully from time to time until fruit is tender and juice has run. Cool and sweeten to taste.

Slice the bread fairly thinly – ¼ inch – and remove crusts. Line the bottom of a soufflé dish or a 4 cup pudding basin, cutting the bread to fit neatly together. Cut more slices in fingers to fit closely round the dish or basin, leaving no gaps. Half fill the dish with fruit, cover with sliced bread, add remaining fruit and cover closely with more bread. Spoon over remaining juice to soak the bread and just fill the dish. Reserve any surplus juice. Fit a small plate into the top of the dish, put on a 2 lb weight and chill overnight.

To unmold, place serving dish on top of basin and invert both together quickly. Carefully lift off the basin. (Use a serving dish which will hold the juice when it runs out.) If there are any little white patches of bread, spoon over the reserved juice. Serve with plain whipped cream.

Poor Knights of Windsor

8 slices French bread, cut about ¼ inch thick
2 whole eggs or 4 yolks
¼ cup sweet sherry
½ cup milk
2 teaspoons sugar
Butter or vegetable oil for frying

For the cinnamon sugar:
2 tablespoons sugar
2 teaspoons ground cinnamon

No one seems to know how these little bread fritters got their curious English name. The original French recipe which came to England in the days of Agincourt was called *Pain Perdu* or *Lost Bread* and it is an excellent way to use up left over French or English bread, dinner rolls or brioches.

Remove the crusts from the bread and lay in a shallow dish. Beat together the eggs, sherry, milk and sugar. Clarify the butter by heating it in a saucepan until it stops bubbling. Remove from heat, allow to settle and strain it slowly through a fine strainer into the frying pan, leaving behind the sediment. This will stop the butter from browning too quickly. Alternatively, use vegetable oil, which does not need clarifying.

Reheat the fat until a piece of dry bread crisps quickly. Pour the egg mixture over the bread, leave a moment and turn over. Lift each slice out on a fish slicer, allow surplus liquid to drip back into the dish, and slide bread into hot fat. Fry until golden underneath, turn and fry other side. Drain on paper towels.

Mix together the sugar and cinnamon, sprinkle thickly on each fritter and serve at once. Children may prefer warm jam or honey.

Variation

Fried jam sandwiches
Convert left over jam sandwiches into a treat for the next day by cutting off the crusts, dipping them in egg and milk and frying them like Poor Knights of Windsor.

Scots Christmas pudding

¾ cup flour
Pinch of salt
1 teaspoon ground allspice
½ teaspoon ground cinnamon
¼ teaspoon ground nutmeg
1½ cups breadcrumbs
⅔ cup brown sugar
¼ lb (1 stick) butter or margarine
1½ cups golden raisins
2 cups dark raisins
½ cup candied mixed peel
1 dessert apple
¼ cup prunes
2½ tablespoons golden or light corn syrup,
warmed
Finely grated rind and juice of 1 small
lemon
2 eggs, beaten
⅓ cup whisky

To finish:
Superfine sugar for dusting
2 tablespoons whisky

Cooking Time: 6 hours

This recipe produces a fruity, spicy pudding of rich dark color, but, by using butter instead of suet the texture is less heavy and more acceptable to young children and many older people. You can use brandy or rum instead of whisky if you prefer.

Sift flour, salt, allspice, ground cinnamon and nutmeg together into a large bowl. Mix in the breadcrumbs and sugar. Rub in the butter. Add the raisins and candied peel. Peel the apple and grate it down to the core, or chop finely, and add to mixture. Roll the prunes between your fingers to soften the flesh and snip them off the pit with scissors – quicker and easier than chopping. Add to the mixture and stir well.

Stir in the golden or light corn syrup, lemon rind and juice, eggs and whisky and mix thoroughly.

Turn into 2 greased 2½ cup pudding basins or one basin double the size. Cover and steam (see page 10) for 6 hours until a rich dark color.

To store
Lift out of steamer and remove covering to prevent condensation from the steam. When cold re-cover with plastic wrap or buttered wax paper. Wrap up in foil, seal carefully and store on a dry, cold shelf. If you want to store the pudding without the basin, allow to shrink slightly and unmold on a large square of buttered foil. When cold, wrap up neatly, sealing well. If you plan to give one of your puddings as a Christmas present, tie it up with red or green ribbon and put a sprig of holly under the bow.

To reheat and serve
Reheat pudding in basin in steamer for 1½–2 hours according to size. Allow to shrink slightly and unmold onto a hot platter. Insert a holly sprig in top and dust lightly with superfine sugar. Heat 2 tablespoons of whisky in a ladle, ignite and pour over pudding. Serve with Whisky or Brandy Butter.

Brandy, whisky or rum butter

¼ lb (1 stick) unsalted butter
2 teaspoons finely grated lemon or orange
rind
½ cup sugar
2–3 tablespoons brandy, whisky or rum

Traditionally served with Christmas pudding and mince pies, this is also called Hard Sauce because after it has been made it is chilled until hard and when served melts deliciously on the hot pudding.

Cream the butter with the grated rind. Add the sugar gradually, 1 tablespoon at a time with 1 teaspoon of brandy, whisky or rum on top of it. By adding the two together the sauce is less likely to curdle. Chill until required. It will keep several days in the refrigerator.

Scots Christmas pudding; Rum butter; Whipped cream

Whipped cream

1 cup heavy cream
Few drops vanilla extract
2 teaspoons sugar

Beat the cream with a fork until it thickens, add the vanilla and sugar to taste and continue beating until soft peaks form. Do not overbeat.

Variation

Fluffy whipped cream
Beat 1 egg white until stiff but not dry and fold into Whipped Cream. It "stretches" the cream twice as far and is delicious served with both hot and cold puddings, hot chocolate and iced coffee.

23

Crispy pear charlotte; Brown Betty

Crispy pear charlotte

1 lb pears (approx. 3)
⅓ cup brown sugar
¼ cup apricot jam
6 slices white bread
¼ lb (1 stick) butter, melted

Cooking Time: 30–40 minutes
Oven: 375°F

Make this attractive variation of the traditional Apple Charlotte when pears are plentiful.
Peel, core and slice the pears. Put half in a well-buttered 5 cup ovenproof dish. Sprinkle with 2 tablespoons sugar and spread with 2 tablespoons jam. Cover with remaining pears, 2 tablespoons sugar and jam.
Remove crusts from the bread and cut each slice into 4 triangles. Dip into melted butter and arrange on top of the pears, covering them completely. Sprinkle with remaining sugar. Bake in moderately hot oven for 30–40 minutes until crisp and golden. Serve hot with plain whipped cream.

Brown Betty

1 lb rhubarb
½ cup sugar
2 cups fresh white breadcrumbs
Finely grated rind and juice of 1 orange
6 tablespoons melted butter

Cooking Time: 45 minutes
Oven: 375°F

The original recipe uses apples, but rhubarb, plums and gooseberries all make excellent Brown Betties.
Wipe the rhubarb and chop into 1 inch lengths. Mix together the sugar, breadcrumbs and orange rind. Butter a 5 cup ovenproof dish and fill with alternate layers of rhubarb and breadcrumbs; sprinkle each layer with melted butter. End with breadcrumbs and butter. Bake in a moderately hot oven for 45 minutes until crisp and golden. Serve hot with plain whipped cream or custard sauce.

Sponge flan

$\frac{1}{4}$ lb (1 stick) butter
$\frac{1}{2}$ cup sugar
2 eggs
$\frac{3}{4}$ cup self-rising flour, sifted
$\frac{1}{4}$ cup apricot jam
$\frac{1}{3}$ cup sliced almonds
Juice of 1 orange
1 lb ripe plums (approx. 10)

To decorate:
$\frac{2}{3}$ cup heavy cream, whipped

Cooking Time: 20 minutes
Oven: 350°F

Cream butter and sugar together until the mixture is light and fluffy. Beat the eggs lightly and add gradually to creamed mixture, beating well between each addition. Fold in the flour quickly and lightly. Turn the mixture into a well-greased 8 inch flan ring. Bake in a preheated moderate oven for 20 minutes or until well risen and golden. Allow to shrink and turn out onto a wire rack. Heat the apricot jam and brush over the border and sides of flan case. Toast the almonds under the broiler, spread on wax paper and roll the flan in them until evenly coated. Spoon orange juice over the inside of the case.
Halve and pit the plums and arrange them overlapping in the flan. Reheat the apricot jam, thin slightly with water if necessary and spoon over fruit. Decorate with the whipped cream.

Points to watch with sponge puddings
1. Soften the fat in a warm place before using but do not heat it, as it may oil and this makes a heavy mixture.
2. Beat the fat with the sugar until pale-colored and fluffy in texture, using a hand mixer or a wooden spoon. Do not leave an electric mixer running too long or the mixture will emulsify, producing a heavy sponge.
3. When beating eggs into the creamed mixture, add very little at a time and beat well between each addition. If the mixture starts to curdle, add a tablespoon of the measured flour each time egg is added. This is nearly always necessary when using an electric mixer.
4. Fold in the sifted flour quickly and lightly about a third at a time. Use a wide spatula; do not beat.
5. Usually extra liquid is needed to produce a soft dropping consistency – the mixture should drop off the wooden spoon by the time you count five.

Sponge flan

Fresh orange sponge

1 orange
2 tablespoons golden or light corn syrup
¼ lb (1 stick) butter or margarine
½ cup sugar
2 eggs
¾ cup flour
2 teaspoons baking powder
1–2 tablespoons warm water

Cooking Time: 1½ hours

This is the lightest of steamed puddings with a delightful fresh orange flavor.
Prepare a steamer saucepan and a greased 4 cup pudding basin.
With a fine grater remove rind from the orange, avoiding the pith, then peel off all pith. Cut the orange into slices, on a plate so as to catch the juice. Spoon the syrup into the bottom of the basin and arrange orange slices on it. Cream the butter and sugar until light and fluffy together with the grated rind. Beat the eggs with a fork and add, a tablespoonful at a time, beating well between each addition. Should the mixture start to curdle, add a spoonful or two of the flour each time egg is added. Sift the flour and baking powder together and fold quickly and lightly into the mixture. Add the orange juice and mix in a tablespoonful or so of warm water to produce a soft dropping consistency (it should fall off the wooden spoon by the time you count five).
Spoon the mixture into the basin on top of the orange slices. Cover with greased foil (see page 10) and put into a steamer. Cover and cook for 1½ hours or so until the pudding is set. To test, remove foil and insert a skewer; it should come out clean. Remove pudding from pan and allow to shrink slightly before turning out onto a warm platter. Serve with Orange Foam Sauce or orange-flavored custard sauce.

Orange foam sauce

2 tablespoons unsalted butter
Finely grated rind and juice of 1 orange
1 tablespoon flour
¼ cup sugar
1 egg, separated
Lemon juice to taste

Cream the butter with the orange rind. Mix the flour and sugar and beat into butter. Add water to the orange juice to make up to ⅔ cup. Add to beaten egg yolk and beat into mixture. Do not worry if it curdles; it will become smooth as it cooks.
Stir the sauce over gentle heat until it thickens and the flour is cooked. Just before serving, beat egg white stiff but not dry and fold into sauce. Sharpen with lemon juice if liked.

Variations

Lemon foam sauce
Substitute lemon rind and juice for orange.

Sherry foam sauce
Substitute ¼ cup sherry for lemon juice but do not omit grated lemon rind.

Raspberry lemon sauce pudding

1½ cups raspberries
2 tablespoons butter
½ cup sugar
Finely grated rind and juice of 1 large
lemon
⅔ cup milk
2 eggs, separated
3 tablespoons flour

Cooking Time: 40–45 minutes
Oven: 375°F

An unusual pudding, this separates during cooking so that it has a light spongy top and a creamy lemon sauce on the raspberries underneath. Make it with any soft fruit or no fruit at all; it is still delicious.

Spread the raspberries over the base of a 2½ cup soufflé dish.

Cream together the butter and 2 tablespoons sugar with the lemon rind. Beat in the lemon juice. Beat the milk into the egg yolks and beat very gradually into the creamed mixture, alternating with flour and remaining sugar until well blended. Beat the egg whites until stiff but not brittle and fold into the lemon mixture.

Pour the pudding mixture over the raspberries and place the dish in a roasting pan with 1 inch of water in the bottom. Cook for 40–45 minutes in a moderately hot preheated oven until the top is golden brown and set. Serve hot with a jug of cream, or cold decorated with piped plain whipped cream and some fresh raspberries.

Fresh orange sponge with orange foam sauce; Raspberry lemon sauce pudding

Prune tutti frutti pudding

⅓ *cup prunes*
½ *cup glacé cherries*
⅓ *cup dried apricots*
¼ *cup angelica*
¼ *lb (1 stick) butter*
½ *cup sugar*
Finely grated rind and juice of 1 lemon
2 eggs
⅔ *cup self-rising flour*
1 cup fresh white breadcrumbs
2 tablespoons apricot jam

Cooking Time: 1½–2 hours

The colorful fruit makes this light steamed sponge pudding look very attractive.

Select 3 large prunes and put in a saucepan with water to cover. Simmer for 10 minutes, then leave to soak.

Snip the flesh off the pits of the remaining prunes with scissors. Halve and set aside 3 large glacé cherries and chop the remainder. Chop the apricots and angelica. Prepare a steamer saucepan and grease a 4 cup pudding basin.

Cream the butter and sugar with the lemon rind until light and fluffy. Beat the eggs, then beat in a little at a time. Mix together the flour and breadcrumbs and fold in lightly. Add the lemon juice and fold in the chopped prunes, cherries, apricots and angelica.

Coat the bottom of the bowl with the apricot jam. Slit the plumped prunes in half, discard pits and arrange on the jam with the halved cherries. Carefully spoon in the pudding mixture.

Cover the bowl with greased foil (see page 10) and steam for 1½–2 hours. Test with a skewer, remove from heat and allow pudding to shrink slightly before unmolding onto a warm platter. Serve with Apricot Jam Sauce (see page 14).

Almond and apricot pudding with apricot sauce

⅓ *cup dried apricots*
2 cups sponge cake crumbs
⅓ *cup ground almonds*
½ *cup light cream*
⅓ *cup milk*
4 tablespoons butter or margarine
¼ *cup sugar*
Finely grated rind of 1 lemon
¼ *teaspoon almond extract*
2 eggs, separated

For the apricot sauce:
¼ *cup dried apricots, cooked*
1 tablespoon cornstarch
1¼ *cups apricot liquid*
1–2 tablespoons sugar
½ *cup light cream*
1–2 teaspoons lemon juice

Cooking Time: 1¾–2 hours

Canned pineapple instead of apricots can be used for this feather-light pudding, and if you have trimmings from sponge finger biscuits left over from another dessert you can use them instead of cake crumbs.

Cover the apricots with 1¼ cups of water, bring to simmering point and cook gently until required.

Put the sponge cake crumbs and ground almonds into a bowl, pour over the cream and milk and leave to soak, stirring occasionally. Cream the butter and sugar with the lemon rind until light and fluffy. Add almond extract to the egg yolks; beat in, alternately with the crumb mixture. Drain, chop and add half the apricots. Beat the egg whites until stiff but not brittle and fold into the mixture. Turn into a well-greased 4 cup pudding mold and cover with well-greased kitchen foil (see page 10). Steam (see page 10) for 1¾–2 hours until well risen. Test with a skewer; it should come out clean. Leave to shrink slightly before unmolding.

Serve hot with Apricot Sauce, made with remaining apricots.

To make the apricot sauce
Drain and sieve the apricots. Put the cornstarch in a small saucepan and gradually blend in the measured apricot liquid and sugar. Bring to the simmer and cook, stirring, for 3 minutes. Cool slightly and gradually add cream. Sweeten to taste and flavor with lemon juice.

Pineapple gâteau; Raspberry and cream jelly roll

Beater sponge puddings

These light, quickly-made sponges are the basis of many desserts.

Points to watch

1. An electric mixer is speedy for beating the eggs and sugar together, but the sifted flour must be folded in by hand, not beaten in by machine, if you want a really light texture. If beating by hand, use a rotary beater or large balloon whisk.
2. The egg and sugar mixture is not ready until it falls off the beater in ribbons which hold their shape on top of the mixture in the bowl for several seconds.
3. Use a wide spatula (see page 6) or large metal spoon to fold in the flour lightly and quickly.

How to line a jelly roll pan

1. Cut a rectangle of wax paper or non-stick parchment 2 inches larger all round than the pan. Grease the bottom of the pan to prevent the paper slipping about.
2. Lay the paper in the pan and using the handle of a metal spoon, press the paper into the angle all round the base of the pan, creasing it firmly.
3. Using scissors, snip the paper from each corner diagonally down to the corner of the pan. Overlap the cut points to fit neatly into the corners of the pan.
4. Brush the wax paper with oil – this is not necessary if using non-stick parchment.

Raspberry and cream jelly roll

3 eggs
Scant ½ cup sugar
⅔ cup flour
1 tablespoon warm water
¼ teaspoon vanilla extract
Sugar for dusting

For the filling:
1½ cups raspberries
1¼ cups heavy cream
2 tablespoons sugar

To decorate:
Angelica leaves or pistachio nuts

Cooking Time: 8–10 minutes
Oven: 425°F

The filling for this delightful summer sweet can be made with strawberries, loganberries or blackberries.

Line a 9 × 12 inch jelly roll pan with wax paper (see opposite). Brush lightly and evenly with oil or melted unsalted butter.

Beat the eggs and sugar together until light and fluffy and the mixture falls off the beater in ribbons. Lightly fold in sifted flour. Mix in water and vanilla extract quickly. Pour mixture into lined pan and spread evenly into corners. Bake near top of preheated hot oven for 8–10 minutes until golden and springy to the touch.

Meanwhile wring out a clean tea towel in hot water. Spread it on the table, place a sheet of wax paper on top and dredge it lightly with sugar.

Turn sponge out upside down on the sugared paper. Carefully ease off edges of lining paper and strip it off. Quickly trim off crisp edges of sponge with a sharp knife. Cut a shallow slit, parallel with the bottom edge and ½ inch above it. Turn bottom edge in neatly for the first roll, then continue to roll with the paper inside. Leave to cool on a wire rack.

Meanwhile crush the raspberries with a fork, reserving a few whole ones for decorating. Whip cream until it forms soft peaks, set some aside for decoration and fold raspberries into the rest. Sweeten to taste.

Unroll sponge, spread with filling and re-roll carefully. Place on a serving plate with join underneath. Whip remaining cream into stiff peaks and pipe onto sponge. Garnish with reserved raspberries and angelica or nuts.

Pineapple gâteau

4 eggs
1 rounded cup sugar
⅓ cup plus 2 teaspoons flour
⅓ cup plus 2 teaspoons potato flour or cornstarch
2 teaspoons baking powder
16 oz can pineapple slices
1¼ cups heavy cream
2 tablespoons Kirsch
1 tablespoon pistachio nuts, chopped

Cooking Time: 20–30 minutes
Oven: 400°F

The sharp tang of the pineapple contrasts agreeably with the sweetness of the sponge in this gâteau, which serves 6–8 people.

Beat the eggs and sugar until mixture falls in ribbons off the beater. Sift together the flour, potato flour and baking powder. Fold a little at a time into the beaten mixture. Turn into an 8 inch greased cake pan. Bake in a preheated moderately hot oven for 20–30 minutes until well risen and springy to the touch. Allow to shrink slightly then turn out onto a wire cooling rack.

Meanwhile drain pineapple slices. Cut half of them into wedges and halve remainder. Whip the cream until stiff. Mix 2 tablespoons of pineapple syrup with the Kirsch. When sponge is cold split in half. Put one half on a serving plate and spoon over pineapple syrup and Kirsch. Arrange pineapple wedges on top and spread with whipped cream. Cover with top half of the sponge. Arrange pineapple half slices on top in a circle, pipe on remaining cream and garnish with pistachio nuts.

Eve's pudding

1 lb cooking apples (3 medium)
½ cup brown sugar
Finely grated rind of 1 lemon
½ cup sugar
¼ lb (1 stick) butter or margarine
¼ teaspoon vanilla extract
2 eggs, beaten
¾ cup self-rising flour
Sugar for dusting

Cooking Time: 35–40 minutes
Oven: 350°F

As one would expect from the name, traditionally there are tempting apples hidden under the sponge topping. But you can vary it very successfully by adding some blackberries, or substituting sliced pears for the apples. In season use gooseberries, rhubarb with grated orange rind, or halved plums or apricots.

Peel, core and slice the apples into a buttered ovenproof dish in layers, sprinkling each layer with brown sugar and grated lemon rind. Cream the white sugar and butter together until light and fluffy. Add the vanilla extract to the eggs and beat in very gradually, adding a little flour if mixture looks like curdling. Fold in the remaining flour and spread the sponge mixture evenly over the fruit.

Bake in a moderate oven for 35–40 minutes until well risen and golden brown. Test the sponge topping with a skewer, which should come out clean. Dust with sugar and serve hot with custard sauce or plain whipped cream.

Black cap castle puddings

⅓ cup blackcurrant jam
¼ lb (1 stick) butter or margarine
½ cup sugar
¼ teaspoon vanilla extract
2 eggs, beaten
¾ cup self-rising flour
1–2 tablespoons warm water

Cooking Time: To bake – 25 minutes; to steam – 50 minutes
Oven: 375°F

Castle puddings are individual sponge puddings which can be baked or steamed and varied in many ways.

Grease 4 dariole molds or custard cups and put 1 teaspoon of blackcurrant jam in the bottom. Cream butter and sugar until light and fluffy. Add vanilla extract to eggs and beat in very gradually, adding a little of the flour if the mixture starts to curdle. Fold in remaining flour. Add 1–2 tablespoons warm water to produce a soft dropping consistency. Fill the molds two-thirds full with mixture, leaving room for the puddings to rise.

To bake :
Place the puddings on a baking tray in a preheated moderate oven for 25 minutes or until well risen and golden brown. Test the puddings with a skewer and when cooked allow to shrink slightly before unmolding. If necessary, trim the tops so that when inverted the puddings will stand level on the serving plate. Serve hot with Blackcurrant Jam Sauce (see page 14) or cold with chilled custard sauce.

To steam :
Place the puddings in a roasting pan with just enough water to come half-way up the molds. Lay a sheet of greased foil on top, but do not tuck tightly round the roasting pan as the steam must be allowed to escape. Cook in a preheated moderate oven for 50 minutes and test with a skewer, which should come out clean. Turn out and serve hot as above with Blackcurrant Jam Sauce or hot custard sauce.

Sticky pear gingerbread

Sticky pear gingerbread

For the topping:
2 firm pears
8 glacé cherries
4 tablespoons unsalted butter
2 tablespoons sugar

For the gingerbread:
¼ lb (1 stick) butter or margarine
½ cup black treacle or molasses
2½ tablespoons golden or light corn syrup
⅓ cup brown sugar
⅔ cup milk
2 eggs, beaten
1¾ cups flour
2 teaspoons ground allspice
2 teaspoons ground ginger
1 teaspoon baking soda

Cooking Time: 1½ hours
Oven: 300°F

This is an old-fashioned sticky gingerbread made by melting the butter and sugar instead of creaming them. It is turned out upside down to reveal slices of pear.

Grease a 7–8 inch cake pan. Peel, core and slice the pears evenly. Arrange the pear slices and the cherries on the base of the pan in a circle. Cream together the butter and sugar and spread over the pears.

Put the butter or margarine, treacle, syrup and brown sugar in a saucepan and heat gradually until melted. Add the milk, cool slightly and stir in the beaten eggs.

Sift together the flour, spices and soda and blend in the egg mixture. Beat smooth and carefully pour over the pears. Bake on the middle shelf of a preheated cool oven for 1½ hours. Test with a skewer; it should come out clean. Allow to shrink before turning out upside down on a serving plate. Serve hot with custard sauce or cold with plain whipped cream.

Viennese caramel pudding

Viennese caramel pudding

$1\frac{1}{4}$ cups milk
$\frac{1}{4}$ cup sugar
2 slices diced brown bread without crust
$\frac{1}{4}$ cup golden raisins
$\frac{1}{2}$ cup glacé cherries, quartered
2 egg yolks
$\frac{1}{2}$ cup light cream
1–2 tablespoons sweet sherry
Lemon juice to taste

For the meringue:
2 egg whites
$\frac{1}{4}$ cup superfine sugar

To decorate:
3 glacé cherries, halved
12 small diamonds of angelica
Superfine sugar

Cooking Time: 50–60 minutes
Oven: 350°F

Heat the milk slowly. Meanwhile make the caramel. Spread the sugar over the base of a thick saucepan, place over gentle heat and stir carefully until dissolved. Increase heat and boil briskly *without stirring*, until it turns a rich caramel color. (If too pale it will not taste of toffee, if too dark it will be bitter.) Remove from heat and pour in about a cupful of milk very gradually, as it will bubble up fiercely. Return to heat and stir until caramel and milk are blended. Stir caramel mixture into remaining milk.

Mix together the diced bread, raisins and cherries, pour over the caramel milk and leave for 20 minutes to swell. Stir in the beaten egg yolks, cream and sherry. Sharpen to taste with lemon juice. Pour into a greased ovenproof dish and bake in the center of a preheated moderate oven for 30 minutes or until set.

Beat the egg whites to a stiff snow and fold in the superfine sugar. Pile on top of pudding, covering carefully. Ruffle or swirl top, decorate with cherries and angelica and sprinkle with sugar. Return to oven for 20 minutes or until crisp and golden. Serve hot or cold.

Note: White bread can be used instead of brown, or, for a sweeter pudding, diced sponge fingers.

Creamy chocolate mold

Scant ⅓ cup cornstarch
¼ cup water
1 large can evaporated milk
3 oz semi-sweet chocolate, grated
1–2 tablespoons sugar

Cooking Time: 5–10 minutes

Mix the cornstarch to a smooth paste with ¼ cup cold water. Heat the evaporated milk, add the chocolate and gradually blend in the cornstarch mixture. Bring to simmering point and cook, stirring, for 3 minutes until thickened. Remove from heat and sweeten to taste.

Rinse a 2½ cup mold with cold water, pour in the mixture and chill. Unmold onto a serving plate and surround with canned or stewed pears.

Note: The chocolate can be replaced by 2 tablespoons cocoa plus ¼ teaspoon vanilla extract and the evaporated milk by 1¼ cups fresh milk plus an equal quantity of light cream.

Lockshen pudding

8 oz egg vermicelli
2 teaspoons salt
4 tablespoons butter
½ cup golden raisins
½ cup candied peel, chopped
¾ cup slivered almonds
¼ teaspoon ground cinnamon
¼ cup sugar
2 eggs, beaten

Cooking Time: 30 minutes
Oven: 350°F

This simple and delicious pudding from Central Europe is traditional in Jewish homes at the Shavours Festival. Drop vermicelli into 2¼ quarts of boiling water with 2 teaspoons salt and cook uncovered for about 5 minutes or until just tender, stirring occasionally. Pour the vermicelli into a colander and drain well. Cut the butter into small pieces. Return the drained vermicelli to the pan. Add the butter and stir gently until melted. Mix in the raisins, candied peel, half the almonds and the cinnamon blended with the sugar. Add the beaten eggs and mix well.

Pour into a buttered ovenproof dish and scatter over the remaining almonds. Bake in a preheated moderate oven for 30 minutes or until set and crisp on top. Serve hot with plain whipped cream.

Sago cream

2½ cups milk
Scant ⅓ cup small sago
¼ teaspoon vanilla extract
¼ cup sugar
½ cup heavy cream
1 egg white
½ teaspoon grated nutmeg

Cooking Time: 20 minutes

Heat the milk in a saucepan, sprinkle on the sago and cook over gentle heat, stirring frequently, for about 20 minutes until sago is soft. Add vanilla, sweeten to taste and pour into a bowl to cool.

Whip the cream until thickened, then the egg white until stiff but not brittle. Fold them together lightly and then into the sago. Turn into a pudding dish or 4 individual bowls or glasses. Sprinkle with nutmeg. Serve cold with Raspberry Jam Sauce (see page 14).

Note: This pudding can also be made with semolina, seed or flaked tapioca. If using whole rice, cook 10 minutes longer.

Spiced semolina

2½ cups milk
Scant ⅓ cup semolina
½ cup sugar
2 teaspoons ground allspice
Finely grated rind of ½ lemon
½ cup golden raisins
2 eggs, separated

Cooking Time: 20 minutes
Oven: 375°F

Heat the milk in a saucepan and sprinkle on the semolina. Bring to the boil, stirring constantly, and cook for a few minutes until the consistency of porridge.

Remove the pan from the heat, stir in 2 tablespoons of sugar, the spice, lemon rind and raisins. Beat the egg yolks with a fork and stir into them 2 tablespoons of the cooked semolina. Blend this mixture into the pudding and pour into a greased ovenproof dish.

Beat the egg whites until stiff and fold in the remaining sugar, reserving a tablespoonful for sprinkling on top. Pile the meringue on the pudding, covering it completely. Swirl or ruffle the top and sprinkle with sugar. Bake on the second shelf of a preheated moderately hot oven for 20 minutes until crisp and golden.

Floating islands with bananas

For the meringues:
2 egg whites
¼ cup superfine sugar

For the custard:
2½ cups milk
2 egg yolks
¼ cup sugar
1 tablespoon cornstarch
¼ teaspoon vanilla extract
2 bananas
2 tablespoons lemon juice

To decorate:
Flaked chocolate

Cooking Time: 30 minutes

Heat the milk for the custard in a wide pan. Beat egg whites until stiff and dry. Sift in half the superfine sugar and beat again until stiff and glossy. Fold in remaining sugar. Scoop up meringue mixture in tablespoons and poach in the hot milk; simmer about 5 minutes until set. Lift out with a draining spoon onto cooking parchment or oiled wax paper to drain.

Beat egg yolks and sugar together until pale lemon color and blend in cornstarch. Gradually mix in the hot milk left from cooking meringues. Pour mixture back into the milk pan and stir over very gentle heat until thickened; do not boil. Add vanilla extract. Slice bananas over the base of a serving bowl, sprinkle with lemon juice and cover with custard. Sprinkle with sugar to prevent a skin forming. Arrange meringues on top and sprinkle them with flaked chocolate. Serve cold.

Orange crème caramel

For the caramel:
½ cup sugar
3 tablespoons water

For the orange custard:
Finely grated rind of 1 orange
1¼ cups fresh or frozen orange juice
3 eggs
3 tablespoons sugar

Cooking Time: 1 hour
Oven: 350°F

Infuse the orange rind in the juice over very gentle heat. Warm 4 ½ cup dariole molds or ramekins in the oven so that the caramel does not set too quickly.

Put the sugar and water into a thick saucepan and stir over gentle heat until dissolved into clear syrup. Boil briskly, *without stirring* until rich caramel color. Divide between molds, and using thick oven mitts as the tins get burning hot, revolve molds so that each is evenly coated. Work quickly before caramel hardens.

Beat eggs and sugar together until light and fluffy. Strain in hot orange juice, mixing well. Pour into prepared molds and put them in a baking pan with 1 inch of water. Cover with greased paper and cook in a preheated moderate oven until set and firm. Chill thoroughly. Unmold into individual dishes; the melted caramel will run down as a delicious sauce.

Floating islands with bananas; Spiced semolina; Orange crème caramel

Crêpe batter

¾ cup flour
¼ teaspoon salt
1 egg
1½ cups milk

This should be the consistency of thin cream – you cannot make delicate thin crêpes with a thick batter. Sift flour and salt into a mixing bowl. Make a well in the center and drop in the egg. Gradually add half the milk, stirring with a wooden spoon from the center and drawing in flour from the sides by degrees. Beat with a rotary beater to ensure the batter is free from lumps and well aerated. Beat in remaining milk. Leave to stand for 20 minutes or longer. This allows flour to swell gradually into the liquid before cooking and produces a smoother, lighter batter. Beat again before using.

To make crêpes
1¼ cups of crêpe batter will make 10–12 crêpes according to size, preferably about 7 inches. Use a thick pan reserved for omelettes and crêpes as it should not be washed, but wiped clean with paper towels or a damp cloth.
Beat up the batter and pour it into a pitcher or bowl with a spout. Heat the pan and grease it lightly. An old-fashioned and very easy way is to rub it with a piece of suet held on a fork; alternatively brush with vegetable oil. Pour off any surplus fat because it will merge with the batter and make the crêpes heavy.
Heat the pan until the fat hazes. Lift it off the burner and pour in just sufficient batter to cover the base of the pan very thinly. Twist and tilt the pan so the batter spreads out evenly. Replace on heat and cook quickly until the crêpe bubbles all over and is golden underneath.
Slip a metal spatula underneath, flip the crêpe over and cook other side. If it lands a little to one side, do not poke it with a knife as it will tear – shake it back into place. When cooked, flick the crêpes out of the pan upside down as the first side cooked should be the outside when it is rolled or folded. Leave the crêpes flat with a piece of wax paper between each if they are to be stored in the refrigerator. If to be frozen, wrap the pile of crêpes in plastic wrap or foil.

Variations

Lemon crêpes
A perennial favorite with both the family and the cook because it is so quick and simple.
As each crêpe is cooked, tip it upside down on a sheet of wax paper dusted with superfine sugar. Sprinkle with lemon juice, lift the nearest edge of the paper and roll the crêpe up. Serve at once.

Caribbean pineapple crêpes
Make 2 thin crêpes for each person. Fill each one with 2 tablespoons heated chopped pineapple, fresh or canned, and sprinkle with brown sugar. Place 2 filled crêpes on each serving plate and dust generously with superfine sugar. Heat a metal skewer and press it in criss-cross pattern onto the sugar which will caramelize in a lattice design. Pour over a spoonful of flaming rum and serve at once.

Normandy crêpes; Lemon crêpes; Caribbean pineapple crêpes

Normandy crêpes

4 medium cooking apples
4 tablespoons unsalted butter
⅓ cup brown or white sugar
8 thin crêpes

For the sauce:
4 tablespoons unsalted butter
¼ cup sugar
⅔ cup cider

To serve:
2 tablespoons Calvados or brandy

Cooking Time: 20 minutes
Oven: 375°F

Delicious apple-stuffed crêpes can be prepared in advance and put in the oven. Calvados (apple brandy) is sold in miniature bottles; if unobtainable use brandy.

Peel, core and cut apples into short slices. Fry in melted butter until just colored. Spoon fried apples down the center of each crêpe and sprinkle with sugar. Fold over the sides of each crêpe and arrange them in a buttered oven dish.

Melt butter and sugar over a moderate heat, add cider and boil briskly for 3–4 minutes. Pour over stuffed crêpes. Bake in moderately hot oven for 20 minutes or until heated through.

Warm Calvados or brandy in a ladle, tilt sideways into a gas flame or use a taper to ignite and pour over crêpes. Serve while flaming. Allow 2 crêpes per helping and serve plain whipped cream separately.

Crêpes Suzette

$\frac{1}{4}$ lb (1 stick) unsalted butter
Finely grated rind and juice of 1 orange
Rounded $\frac{1}{2}$ cup sugar
8 thin crêpes
2 tablespoons Orange
Curaçao, Cointreau or Grand Marnier
2 tablespoons brandy

Thin lacy crêpes flamed in an orange liqueur sauce are a favorite choice when dining out, but they can be happily accomplished at home by the host or hostess cook who follows this method, as the crêpes and the Suzette Butter can be prepared in advance.

Cream the butter with the orange rind. Add the sugar, a tablespoonful at a time, pouring a little orange juice on the butter, and beat both in together to prevent the liquid separating from the fat. Stop adding juice when it starts to curdle. The Suzette Butter can be prepared in advance and refrigerated or frozen until required.

When you are ready to serve, heat the Suzette Butter gently in a chafing dish or frying pan (this can be done on a side table in the dining room) and put the crêpes in one at a time, spooning the sauce over them. Fold each crêpe in half and then in half again, push to the side of the pan and put in the next one.

When all the crêpes are folded and the sauce slightly reduced and thickened, pour over the orange liqueur. Warm the brandy in a ladle or small pan, tilt into the flame so that it ignites and pour over the crêpes. Shake the pan to liven the flames. Serve two crêpes for each helping and spoon on more sauce.

Prune and apricot snowballs

8 large prunes (soaked overnight)
8 dried apricots (soaked overnight)
3 tablespoons butter or margarine
⅔ cup water
⅔ cup flour, sifted
2 eggs, beaten
Deep fat for frying
Crystallized ginger; or glacé cherries; or blanched almonds
⅓–⅔ cup confectioners' sugar, sifted

Little choux pastry fritters are filled with prunes or apricots stuffed with crystallized ginger, glacé cherries or blanched almonds. One-third cup of sherry added to the soaking water for the fruit improves the flavor.

Remove the prunes and apricots from the soaking liquid, slit down one side, remove prune pits and leave fruit to drain.

Melt the butter in the water over gentle heat, then bring to the boil and toss in the flour. Beat well with a wooden spoon over moderate heat until the dough forms a smooth ball. Add the beaten egg *very* gradually, beating well between each addition.

Stuff the drained fruit with a knob of ginger, a glacé cherry or a blanched almond and press firmly together. Heat fat to 375°F. You can test it by dropping in a teaspoon of dough, which should rise at once to the surface and start to crisp. Take up tablespoons of the dough and drop them carefully into the hot fat. Use a teaspoon to push the dough off the tablespoon. Fry until puffed up, golden and crisp.

As each one is ready, remove from the fat with a slotted spoon, slit and stuff hollow center with the stuffed fruit. Roll in the confectioners' sugar and keep warm. Serve at once.

Greek almond fritters

⅓ cup ground almonds
2 tablespoons sugar
¼ teaspoon ground cinnamon
2–3 teaspoons lemon juice
½ batch plain shortcrust pastry (see page 48)
Deep fat for frying
¼ cup honey
2 tablespoons orange juice

Mix the almonds, sugar and cinnamon. Add the lemon juice and mix together well. Roll out the pastry very thinly and cut into 3 inch squares. Put a small piece of filling in the center of each square, dampen the edges and fold over into triangles; press edges firmly together.

Heat the fat to 375°F (a piece of dough dropped in should rise and crisp quickly). Fry the fritters a few at a time until golden all over. Drain on paper towels and keep warm while frying the next batch.

Heat the honey and orange juice together and dip in each fritter, coating it well. Serve hot as soon as possible. For parties you can make and fry the fritters in advance. Reheat them in a moderately hot oven and dip them into the orange honey syrup just before serving.

Vary the filling by using ground walnuts instead of almonds, or slit and seeded grapes.

Prune and apricot snowballs; Fluffy fruit fritters; Greek almond fritters

Fluffy fruit fritters

¾ *cup flour*
Pinch of salt
1 tablespoon corn oil
About ⅔ cup tepid water
2 egg whites
4 bananas, quartered; or 12 apple rings;
or 12 pineapple rings
Deep fat for frying
Sugar for dusting
1 lemon

Fruit fritters can be made with the basic crêpe batter using ⅔ cup milk to ¾ cup flour but this continental recipe gives a lighter, crisper result.

Sift the flour and salt into a bowl and make a well in the center. Add the oil to the water and pour this liquid gradually into the well, stirring in the flour from the sides by degrees. When all the flour is incorporated add just sufficient liquid to make the batter coat the back of the wooden spoon. Beat well with a rotary beater to ensure that the batter is free from lumps and well aerated. Allow to stand for 20 minutes or more for the flour to swell.

When ready to cook the fritters beat the egg whites until stiff but not brittle and fold into the batter.

Heat the fat to 375°F. (You can test it by dropping in a teaspoonful of batter, which will rise quickly and crisp if fat is the right temperature.) Using cooking tongs, dip pieces of fruit, one at a time, into batter, coat completely and draw over the rim of the bowl to allow surplus batter to run back. Lower carefully into hot fat. Do not try to fry too many fritters at once.

Watch the temperature of the fat between batches; if too low fritters will be greasy, if too hot they will burn. When a fritter is golden underneath, turn and fry other side. Remove from fat and drain on paper towels. Sprinkle with sugar and serve with lemon wedges.

Fruity griddle cakes

2 eggs, separated
¾ cup flour
2 teaspoons baking powder
2 tablespoons sugar
⅔ cup milk
1 tablespoon melted butter
2 apples or 2 bananas

To serve:
Warmed honey, maple syrup or lemon juice

For a quick and easy last-minute pudding Griddle Cakes are winners and handy for boating and sailing holidays. You can use a thick frying pan if you have no griddle.

Beat the egg whites until stiff. Sift the flour, baking powder and 1 tablespoon sugar into a bowl. Beat the egg yolks lightly and mix in with the milk and melted butter. Peel and coarsely grate the apples, discarding the core; or peel and chop bananas. Fold the fruit into the batter and then the beaten egg whites.

Heat the griddle or frying pan and grease lightly. It is hot enough when a drop of water spits and splutters. Drop the batter on the hot griddle in tablespoons, allowing room for spreading. In a minute or two, when puffed and bubbly, flip over and brown the other side. Sprinkle with remaining sugar and serve with warmed honey, maple syrup or fresh lemon juice.

Cherry Clafoutis

1 lb ripe cherries
2 eggs, beaten
⅓ cup plus 2 teaspoons flour, sifted
¼ cup sugar
1¼ cups milk, warmed
1 tablespoon cherry brandy (optional)
2 tablespoons butter, melted
Superfine sugar for dusting

Cooking Time: 40 minutes
Oven: 400°F, then reduce to 375°F

This is a French country dish from Limousin where they pour the batter over the juicy black cherries of the region. In winter use drained canned cherries.

Butter a shallow 2½ cup ovenproof dish. An 8 inch French pottery flan dish is ideal. Stem and pit the cherries. Beat eggs and gradually blend in flour and sugar. Slowly add warm milk, beating steadily. Add cherry brandy if using and beat in melted butter. Spread the prepared cherries over the base of the dish and pour the batter over them.

Bake in the center of preheated oven for 20 minutes, then reduce heat slightly and continue cooking for 20 minutes or until the batter is well risen, golden and set. Serve hot, generously dusted with superfine sugar.

Butterscotch upside down pudding

4 pineapple rings
4 cherries
⅔ cup brown sugar
4 tablespoons butter or margarine
¼ cup chopped walnuts

For the batter:
2 eggs, separated
¼ teaspoon vanilla extract
1 tablespoon melted butter
½ cup sugar
¾ cup flour
1 teaspoon baking powder

Cooking Time: 30 minutes
Oven: 325°F

Vary the fruit topping for this pudding by using apple rings, sliced pears or orange segments.

Grease an 8 inch shallow cake pan and arrange the pineapple slices on the bottom with a cherry in the center of each. Dissolve the sugar and melt the butter in a saucepan over gentle heat, then stir in the nuts. Mix well and pour over the pineapple slices.

Beat the egg yolks with the vanilla and melted butter until creamy. Beat the egg whites until stiff but not brittle and fold in the sugar and the egg yolk mixture. Sift together the flour and baking powder and fold in carefully. Pour the batter into the pan and spread it evenly. Bake in a preheated warm oven for 30 minutes or until firm and golden. Turn out upside down on a platter and serve hot or cold with plain whipped cream.

Cherry Clafoutis; Fruity griddle cakes; Butterscotch upside down pudding

Plain shortcrust pastry

1¾ cups flour
Pinch of salt
¼ lb (1 stick or ½ cup) butter, margarine,
lard or shortening
Cold water to mix

Making pastry
There are some golden rules for all pastries. Use cold ingredients, cold steel to mix and cold fingers to handle the dough. Sift and aerate the flour. Rub in fat lightly with finger tips – don't squeeze it into marzipan. Add liquid carefully as too much makes heavy dough, too little makes it crumbly and difficult to roll out. Use short, firm rolls, lifting the pin frequently. Don't steam-roller out the air in the pastry or work in too much flour from the board. If sticky, chill before using.

This unsweetened pastry is quick and easy to make and does not need to be rested after mixing but can be used at once, either for baking or frying. Use either plain or self-rising flour, with butter, margarine, lard or vegetable shortening.

Sift the flour and salt into a mixing bowl. Cut the fat into the flour and toss until well covered. Now rub it in with the tips of the fingers, lifting your hands well above the bowl to incorporate plenty of air.

When the mixture resembles breadcrumbs, shake the bowl and rub in any lumps which come to the surface. Add the cold water a little at a time, stirring with a metal spatula, until the mixture begins to bind. Now gather it up with your fingers and work it into a soft but not sticky dough, leaving the bowl clean. Do not over-knead it as it will become too elastic.

Spiced pear pie

Plain shortcrust pastry (see above)
3 tablespoons sugar
¼ cup brown sugar
1 tablespoon flour
¼ teaspoon grated nutmeg
¼ teaspoon ground cinnamon
Finely grated rind and juice of 1 orange
Finely grated rind of ½ lemon
1 tablespoon lemon juice
2 lb cooking pears
½ cup golden raisins
3 tablespoons butter, melted

To glaze:
Milk
Sugar

Cooking Time: 45 minutes
Oven: 400°F, then reduce to 375°F

An exciting blend of flavors distinguish the filling of this double crust pie. The same recipe is excellent made with apples.

Light the oven and grease the base of an 8 inch round shallow pie dish. Moisten the lip of the dish.

Divide the pastry in half. Roll out one half thinly, line the pie dish and prick all over the base. Mix together the sugars, flour and spices. Rub a little of the mixture over the pastry lining. Add the grated orange and lemon rind to the remainder.

Peel, core and slice the pears. Arrange them in layers in the dish, sprinkling each layer with raisins, sugar mixture, fruit juices and melted butter.

Roll out the other piece of dough into a circle about 2 inches larger all round than the top of the pie. Moisten the edge of the lining pastry, lift the other piece on the rolling pin and unroll it across the top of the pie.

Press the two edges firmly together and with a sharp knife trim off the surplus dough. Knock the two edges together with the back of the knife and flute the edge. Make a few slits in the top of the pie to allow the steam from the fruit to escape. Brush lightly with milk and sprinkle with sugar to give a glazed finish.

Bake in a moderately hot oven for 20 minutes until the pastry is well risen and turning color; lower the heat and continue baking for 25 minutes or until the pie is cooked through. Serve hot with plain whipped cream.

Treacle tart; Spiced pear pie

Treacle tart

*Plain shortcrust pastry made with $1\frac{1}{3}$
cups flour and 6 tablespoons fat
(see opposite)*
*3 rounded tablespoons golden or light
corn syrup*
1 teaspoon finely grated lemon rind
*2 rounded tablespoons fresh white
breadcrumbs*

Cooking Time: 30–35 minutes
Oven: 375°F

Grease the base, but not the lip, of an 8 inch ovenproof plate
or shallow pie dish. Roll the pastry out thinly into a circle.
Cut strips off the outside edge the same width as the lip of the
plate. Dampen the lip and press on the pastry strip; dampen
the strip. Roll remaining pastry over the pin and unroll over the
plate, ease it into the base of the plate and press outer edges
firmly together. Trim off surplus pastry, knock-up outside edge
with the back of a knife and flute it. Prick bottom of tart all over
with a fork.
Warm the syrup with the lemon rind, mix in the breadcrumbs and
pour into the tart. Cut pastry trimmings into narrow strips and
criss-cross lattice fashion over the filling. Dampen the ends of
the strips and fix firmly on to pastry edge. Cover with little
circles cut out of trimmings. Bake in the center of preheated
moderately hot oven for 30 minutes or until the pastry is crisp and
golden. Serve hot or cold.

49

Sweet shortcrust pastry

1⅓ cups flour
Pinch of salt
4 tablespoons butter or margarine
¼ cup lard or shortening
2 teaspoons sugar
1 egg yolk, beaten
Cold water to mix

This quantity is sufficient to line a flan case measuring 8–9 inches across.
Sift the flour and salt into a mixing bowl. Cut in the fat and toss until covered with flour. Rub in the fat with the tips of the fingers, lifting your hands well above the bowl to incorporate as much air as possible. Add the sugar and mix thoroughly.
Stir a tablespoon of water into the egg yolk and mix into the pastry. Stir in sufficient cold water, using a metal spatula to make a fairly stiff dough. Turn onto a floured board and knead lightly to remove cracks. Cover and put into the refrigerator to relax for at least 30 minutes before rolling out.

Grapefruit meringue pie

1 shortcrust flan case (7–8 in)
baked blind
2 tablespoons cornstarch
1 cup grapefruit juice
About ½ cup sugar
2 egg yolks, beaten

For the meringue:
2 egg whites
¼ cup superfine sugar, sifted
Superfine sugar for dusting

Cooking Time: 30 minutes
Oven: 325°F

This is a variation of the ever-popular Lemon Meringue Pie. You can use the small inexpensive fresh grapefruit or canned or frozen juice, which must be unsweetened to give the characteristic contrast of sharp filling and sweet topping. The pie case can be made with plain or sweet shortcrust (see page 48 and above).
Blend the cornstarch with a little of the grapefruit juice to a smooth paste in a small saucepan. Gradually stir in remaining juice. Heat gradually, stirring continuously with a wooden spoon, then simmer gently for 3 minutes or until the mixture thickens and clears. Remove from heat and sweeten to taste. Cool slightly and gradually beat in the egg yolks. Pour into the pie case and smooth the top.
To make the meringue, beat the egg whites until very stiff and dry. Fold in the sugar quickly and lightly. Spoon the meringue mixture round the outside edge of the pie and work towards the center. Make sure the filling is completely covered and there are no little gaps round the pastry edge or the meringue will "weep". Dust with sugar. Bake in the center of a preheated moderate oven for 25–30 minutes or until set and golden colored. Serve hot or cold, decorated with sugared grapefruit peel if available.

How to line a flan ring; How to bake blind; Grapefruit meringue pie

To line a flan ring

1. Place the ungreased flan ring on a greased baking sheet. Roll out the pastry with quick jerky rolls into a circle about $\frac{1}{4}$ inch thick which will extend $1\frac{1}{2}$ inches beyond the flan ring all round.
2. Raise the pastry circle off the board and drop it gently back so that it can shrink before, and not during, cooking. Fold the pastry into a 5-sided shape small enough to fit inside the ring.
3. Lift it into the flan ring, open it out carefully easing (never stretching) it into the angle all round the base and press the pastry into the flutes with a floured finger.
4. Roll the rolling pin across the top of the flan ring to cut off the surplus pastry. Remove the trimmings.

To bake a flan case blind

1. Prick the base of the flan all over through to the baking sheet. Line with a piece of wax or buttered paper and cover with a layer of dried beans to keep the pastry flat during cooking.
2. Bake in a preheated moderately hot oven (400°F) for 15–20 minutes until the sides of the flan are set and crisp. Remove from the oven, lift out paper and beans (which you can use again) and return flan to oven for 5 minutes to crisp the base.
3. When removed from oven, allow the pastry to shrink slightly before lifting off the flan ring. Never lift flan up by the sides; slide a fish slicer or wide spatula underneath.

Orange honey gingernut pie

6 oz ginger nuts (approx. 3 cups)
¼ cup sugar
4 tablespoons butter, melted

For the filling:
1 cup cottage cheese
⅔ cup plain yogurt
1 tablespoon orange blossom honey
Finely grated rind and juice of 1 large
orange
2 teaspoons powdered gelatin
3 tablespoons hot water

To decorate:
½ cup heavy cream
5 crystallized orange slices

The crunchy crust on this pie contrasts with the smooth sweet filling which is fresh and delicate in flavor, especially if you use a blossom-flavored honey such as orange, heather or clover.

Crush the ginger nuts between 2 sheets of wax paper with a rolling pin, or use an electric blender. Combine with sugar and melted butter. Press into an 8 inch pottery flan dish or shallow pie dish. Chill until firm in refrigerator.

Sieve the cottage cheese into a bowl and mix in yogurt and honey. Add the orange rind and juice. Dissolve the gelatin thoroughly in the hot water and stir into the mixture. Pour into the pie case and chill in refrigerator until set.

Decorate with piped whipped cream and crystallized orange slices cut into wedges.

Kentucky raisin pie

Sweet shortcrust pastry (see page 50)
1¼ cups dark raisins
¼ teaspoon baking soda
¼ cup hot water
⅓ cup brown sugar

For the topping:
¾ cup flour
½ teaspoon ground cinnamon
¼ teaspoon ground nutmeg
¼ teaspoon ground ginger
4 tablespoons butter
⅓ cup brown sugar

Cooking Time: 30 minutes
Oven: 425°F, then reduce to 325°F

A sugar-and-spice pie which is a favorite with "sweet tooths" of all ages.

Roll out the pastry thinly and line an 8 inch greased pie plate. Pinch the edge of the pastry with finger and thumb into a decorative border. Prick the pastry base all over through to the plate and cover with raisins. Mix the baking soda with the water and the brown sugar and pour it over the raisins.

Sift the flour and spices together. Cut in the butter and rub it in with the tips of the fingers until the consistency of breadcrumbs. Mix in the sugar and spread over the raisin filling.

Bake in a preheated hot oven for 10 minutes until the pie begins to brown. Reduce the heat and continue cooking for 20 minutes until the filling is set. Serve hot or cold, with plain whipped cream if wished.

Harlequin jam tart

Plain shortcrust pastry (see page 48)
1 tablespoon raspberry jam
1 tablespoon apricot jam
1 tablespoon gooseberry jam
1 tablespoon blackberry jam

Cooking Time: 30 minutes
Oven: 375°F

Roll the pastry out thinly and line an 8 inch pie plate as for Treacle Tart (see page 49). With a knife mark the bottom pastry across into 8 equal triangles. Spread each triangle with jam, alternating the colors.

Cut the pastry trimmings into narrow strips and arrange them across the tart, dividing the jams. Dampen the end of each strip, press one end on the pastry edge, twist it across the tart and secure on the other side. Cover the ends with cut out pastry shapes.

Bake in the center of preheated moderately hot oven for 30 minutes.

Norfolk treacle custard tart

½ batch plain shortcrust pastry
(see page 48)
¼ cup golden or light corn syrup
1 teaspoon finely grated lemon rind
1 tablespoon butter
2 tablespoons light cream
1 egg, beaten

Cooking Time: 40 minutes
Oven: 350°F

Roll pastry out thinly and line an 8 inch flan ring (see page 51). Prick the bottom. Warm the syrup with the lemon rind. Cut the butter into small pieces and stir it into the syrup. Beat the cream and egg together and blend into the syrup. Pour into the flan case. Bake in the center of a moderate oven for 40 minutes or until pastry is crisp and filling is set. Allow to shrink before removing flan ring and slide onto a serving plate. Serve hot or cold.

Orange honey gingernut pie; Kentucky raisin pie; Harlequin jam tart; Norfolk treacle custard tart

Cherry brandy pie

2 lb cherries, pitted
Scant ½ cup sugar
Plain or sweet shortcrust pastry (see
page 48 or 50)
¼ cup Cherry Brandy
½ cup heavy cream, warmed
Superfine sugar for dusting

Cooking Time: 45 minutes
Oven: 400°F, then reduce to 375°F

This is a party version of fruit pie, with cream and liqueur poured in under the lid. In Normandy they make it with apples and use Calvados (apple brandy).

Light the oven. Fill a 4 cup oval pie dish with the pitted cherries, sugaring each layer.

Roll out the pastry thinly in an oval, 2 inches wider than the top of the dish all round. Cut a strip of pastry, the same width as the lip of the dish, off the outside edge of the pastry. Dampen the lip and press pastry strip firmly down on it. Dampen the pastry strip, lift the rest of the pastry on the rolling pin and unroll it over the dish. Press the pastry edges together and trim off the surplus with a sharp knife. Holding the knife horizontally and using the back of it, knock up the pastry edge. Keep the thumb or crooked forefinger of the other hand on the pie, so the pastry is kept firmly pressed to the lip of the dish. Mark the outer edge neatly with the tines of a fork or flute it. Prick the top to allow the steam to escape.

Bake in the preheated moderately hot oven for 20 minutes, then reduce heat and continue cooking for 25 minutes until the fruit is cooked.

Remove from oven and cut neatly round the lid of the pie just inside the lip; lift off carefully. Pour the cherry brandy over the fruit and then the cream. Replace the lid, dust with sugar and return to the oven for 5 minutes. Serve hot.

Coffee and walnut pie

Sweet shortcrust pastry (see page 50)
2 tablespoons apricot jam
6 tablespoons butter
Scant ½ cup sugar
1 egg, beaten
⅓ cup walnuts, finely chopped
¾ cup self-rising flour
4 teaspoons instant coffee powder
1 tablespoon milk
⅔ cup sour cream

To decorate:
Walnuts, coarsely chopped

Cooking Time: 45 minutes
Oven: 425°F, then reduce to 325°F

Roll out pastry and line an 8 inch flan ring. Prick base and spread with apricot jam. Cream butter and sugar together until light and fluffy; gradually beat in egg. Fold in walnuts and flour. Dissolve the coffee in the milk. Heat if necessary but allow to cool, then blend into mixture. Turn into pie case and smooth top.

Bake in the center of preheated hot oven for 15 minutes. Reduce heat to moderate and bake for an additional 25 minutes or until cooked; test with a skewer which should come out clean. Warm sour cream, but do not overheat. Pour over pie and return to oven for 5 minutes. Remove from the oven, scatter chopped walnuts on top and serve immediately.

This pie is also very good served cold: spread lemon-flavored glacé icing over the filling instead of the sour cream and decorate with walnut halves.

Winter fruit salad

For the salad:
½ cup dried apricots
½ cup prunes or dried pears
½ cup dried peaches
½ cup dried apple rings
¼ lb green grapes, seeded

For the syrup:
2½ cups dried fruit liquid
¾ cup sugar
1 thin sliver lemon rind

Dried fruit, nicely prepared, makes an excellent compote or salad. You can also mix in fresh fruit available in winter, such as orange sections or green grapes.

Put the dried fruit in a large bowl, cover with 5 cups of water and soak overnight.

Measure off 2½ cups of the liquid, add the sugar and lemon rind and make syrup as below. Drain fruit, add to prepared syrup and simmer gently for 20 minutes. Mix in seeded green grapes.

Serve hot or well-chilled with Lemon Flummery, plain whipped cream or custard sauce.

To make syrup for fruit salad
According to the sweetness required, use ¾-1½ cups of sugar to 2½ cups of water or dried fruit liquid. Add a thin sliver of lemon or orange rind, a vanilla bean, a stick of cinnamon or a blade of mace for flavor. Boil briskly for about 5 minutes, reduce heat and add the fruit, which should be just covered. You can also flavor with rum, sherry or liqueur.

Lemon flummery

1¼ cups water
2 tablespoons butter
Finely grated rind and juice of 1 lemon
3 tablespoons flour
½ cup sugar
1 egg, separated

Heat the water with the butter and lemon rind. Mix the flour and sugar in a bowl. Gradually stir in the hot liquid, beating smooth. Blend a little of this mixture into the beaten egg yolk. Mix this back into the mixture and pour all back into the saucepan. Cook gently for 5 minutes. Add the lemon juice and pour into a cold bowl. Beat the egg white until stiff but not dry and fold into the flummery. Serve hot or cold with baked fruit, fruit compotes, etc.

Fluffy fruit fool

⅔ cup milk
2 eggs, separated
1¼ cups sweetened rhubarb purée
(see opposite)
⅔ cup heavy cream
Sugar to taste

Fruit fools are easily made. Usually they consist of fruit purée blended with cornstarch or a simple milk and egg yolk custard and/or whipped cream. In this recipe beaten egg whites are also folded into the fool which gives it a lighter texture and makes it suitable for freezing.

Warm the milk and add gradually to the beaten egg yolks. Pour back into the rinsed saucepan. Stir over gentle heat until the mixture thickens and clings to the back of the wooden spoon. Chill thoroughly and mix into the rhubarb purée. Whip the cream fairly stiff and fold in. Sweeten to taste. Beat the egg whites until stiff but not brittle and fold into the fool. Pour into goblets and chill until required. Serve topped with baby meringues or ratafias; accompany with cookies or ladyfingers.

Lemon flummery; Winter fruit salad; Fluffy fruit fool

Fruit purée

Fruit purée is an important ingredient in many desserts. If it is thin and watery it will spoil the dish; it must be thick and full of flavor. The fruit can be cooked in a saucepan on top of the stove, or in a casserole in a moderate oven (350°F). Do not add sugar until the fruit is cooked as it will toughen the skins. One pound of fresh fruit yields about $1\frac{1}{4}$ cups of purée.

Apricots, plums
Wash under running cold water. Cut round the fruit in the natural crease down to the pit. Twist the two halves in opposite directions so that the fruit splits and the pits can be removed. Cover the base of a thick saucepan with water. Add the fruit and cook gently until juice runs. Remove lid and continue cooking until liquid has evaporated. Sieve fruit or mash in a blender. Sweeten to taste.

Raspberries, loganberries, strawberries
These do not need to be cooked to make a purée, but must be strained if you want to get rid of the pips.

Apples
Quarter, peel thinly, remove cores and slice into a bowl of cold water with 2 tablespoons of lemon juice to prevent discoloration. Butter the bottom of a thick saucepan. Put in the drained apples and 2 tablespoons water. Cover and cook gently until juice begins to flow. Remove lid and continue cooking until apples are soft and liquid has evaporated, stirring gently from time to time. Beat into a smooth thick purée with a wooden spoon. Add sugar to taste.

Gooseberries, blackberries, redcurrants
Top and tail the fruit with scissors. Wash under running cold water and cook as apricots.

Rhubarb
Cut off the leaves (which contain unwholesome oxalic acid), and the thick white ends of the stalks. Wash or wipe the stalks clean and chop into 1 inch lengths. Put into a buttered pan with a sliver of orange rind or two tablespoons orange juice and cook as apples.

57

Berries with cointreau chantilly

1 pint strawberries
1½ cups heavy cream
2 tablespoons sugar
1–2 tablespoons Cointreau

To decorate:
Crushed meringues or ratafias
Crystallized mint leaves

Hull the strawberries. Whip the cream until stiff and fold in the sugar. Flavor to taste with Cointreau. Fold in the prepared berries and spoon into individual glasses. Chill until required.

Serve topped with crushed meringues or ratafias and garnished with crystallized mint leaves.

Strawberries, raspberries, loganberries or cultivated blackberries can all be used in this quickly-prepared and delicious sweet. Flavor with Cointreau, Grand Marnier, Orange Curaçao or Kirsch according to taste and availability.

Honeydew and pineapple basket

1 ripe honeydew melon
4 slices pineapple, fresh or canned
3–4 tablespoons condensed milk (sweet)
⅓ cup ground almonds
1 tablespoon lemon juice

Cut top third off melon and discard seeds. Scoop flesh out of both parts with a sharp spoon and cut in pieces. Trim the edges of melon shells by cutting small triangles all around to give a zig-zag effect.

Chop the pineapple and mix with melon flesh, condensed milk, ground almonds and lemon juice. Pack this mixture into larger melon shell and pile it up in the center. Put melon lid on at an angle and secure at back with cocktail sticks. Wrap melon completely in plastic wrap or foil and chill thoroughly. Serve garnished with fresh leaves and/or flowers and crushed ice.

French apple and ginger cake

1 cup sugar
⅔ cup cider
⅔ cup water
2 tablespoons ginger syrup
Piece of thin lemon rind
2 lb dessert apples
½ cup golden raisins
½ cup chopped preserved ginger

To decorate:
⅔ cup heavy cream
Preserved ginger

This dessert should be made well in advance so that it can be thoroughly chilled, preferably overnight. It is also very good made with pears. Use ginger preserved in syrup, not the sugary crystallized ginger.

Line the base of a 7–8 inch cake pan with foil and brush all over lightly with oil.

Dissolve the sugar in the cider and water, add the ginger syrup and lemon rind and bring to the boil. Wash and core the apples, slice thinly and add to the syrup. Simmer very gently, without a lid, until the apple slices are transparent. Stir occasionally, taking care not to break the slices.

When the apple slices are cooked, lift them out of the syrup with a draining spoon and arrange in layers in the pan, sprinkling each layer with raisins and chopped ginger. When all the apple is in, cover with a heavy oiled plate which fits in the top of the pan. Chill in the refrigerator, preferably overnight.

To serve remove plate and place a large platter over the pan. Invert both together quickly, and carefully remove the pan and foil. Decorate the cake with piped whipped cream and preserved ginger.

Apricot amber; Flamed Jamaican bananas

Apricot amber

1¼ cups sweetened apricot
purée, still warm (see page 57)
Lemon juice to taste
2 tablespoons butter
2 eggs, separated
¼ cup superfine sugar
Superfine sugar for dusting

Cooking Time: 30–35 minutes
Oven: 325°F

Sharpen the purée to taste with lemon juice. Stir in the butter and beaten egg yolks. Pour the mixture into a greased shallow pie dish. Beat the egg whites to a stiff snow and fold in the superfine sugar. Cover the fruit mixture completely with the meringue and ruffle the top. Dust with sugar. Bake in the center of a warm oven for 30 minutes or until meringue is crisp and golden. Serve hot or cold.
You can make this pudding equally well with any fruit purée. For a more hearty dish bake in a shortcrust pastry case (see pages 48 or 50).

Flamed Jamaican bananas

4 large under-ripe bananas
3 tablespoons butter
Juice of ½ large lemon
2 tablespoons rum

To serve:
Brown sugar
Heavy cream

Peel the bananas and halve lengthwise. Heat the butter in a flameproof dish and fry the bananas, cut side down. When golden, turn over, sprinkle with lemon juice, and fry until the underneath is coloring. Warm the rum in a ladle, ignite and pour over bananas. Serve while still flaming with a bowl of brown sugar and a jug of cream. If no flameproof dish is available use a frying pan.

Fresh pineapple pyramid

Fresh pineapple pyramid

1 medium pineapple
3–4 tablespoons sugar
¾ cup heavy cream
2 tablespoons Kirsch (optional)
¾–1 pint strawberries; or raspberries; or cherries

This fresh fruit dessert makes an attractive dish on buffet or dinner tables. Be sure to choose a pineapple with a top of fresh green leaves. In winter orange or mandarin sections can replace the summer fruit.

Cut the top off the pineapple complete with leaves and set aside. Level off the bottom and discard the fibrous base. Stand the pineapple on a chopping board and with a large sharp knife, working downwards from the top, cut off the skin all round. Cut the pineapple across in thick slices – ½ inch. Remove the core from each slice with an apple corer and sprinkle with sugar. Whip the cream stiffly, sweeten to taste and add Kirsch if using. Hull and halve the strawberries, pick over the raspberries or pit the cherries.

Reform the pineapple in an upright position on a serving platter, spreading a layer of cream covered with prepared fruit between each slice. Replace the top, with leaves, wrap in plastic wrap and refrigerate until required. When serving use a pastry slice to remove top and serve one slice complete with whipped cream and strawberries to each guest.

Hot chocolate soufflé

¼ lb semi-sweet chocolate
¼ cup strong black coffee
3 tablespoons butter
4 tablespoons flour
1 cup milk
¼ cup sugar
¼ teaspoon vanilla extract
3 egg yolks
4 egg whites
Confectioners' sugar to glaze

To serve:
⅔ cup light cream
2–3 tablespoons rum or Tia Maria

Cooking Time: 25–30 minutes
Oven: 375°F

Chocolate is a rich, rather heavy ingredient and it is essential to use an extra egg white in this soufflé to get a really light, fluffy texture.

Prepare a 6 inch soufflé dish and the oven (see below). Break up chocolate and put in a bowl with the black coffee over a saucepan of hot water to melt.

Melt butter in a small saucepan, remove from heat and blend in flour. Gradually add milk, bring to the boil and simmer, stirring, for 3 minutes. Stir melted chocolate until smooth and blend into the sauce. Stir in sugar until dissolved and the vanilla. Remove from heat, cool slightly and gradually beat in egg yolks.

Beat the egg whites until stiff but not brittle, in a large bowl. Pour over the chocolate mixture, about a third at a time, and fold it in quickly and lightly.

Pour into a prepared soufflé dish. With a teaspoon dig a little trench, about ½ inch deep, about 1 inch from the rim of the dish all round. This will give a "crown" to the soufflé when it rises.

When the soufflé has baked for 25 minutes, draw the oven shelf forward, dust with confectioners' sugar and return to the oven for 5 minutes to caramelize. Serve immediately with cream flavored with rum or Tia Maria. The liqueur can be added to the soufflé mixture, but as it is very volatile in hot mixtures it will have more effect in the cream.

To prepare a soufflé dish
Choose the right size so the soufflé can rise well above the dish. For a 2-egg soufflé, use a 5 inch dish; for a 3-egg soufflé a 6 inch dish and for a 4-egg soufflé a 7 inch dish. Cut a band of double wax paper long enough to overlap by 2 inches round the dish and wide enough to stand 3 inches above it. Grease the inside of the dish and the top half of the paper band. Wrap it round the outside of the dish with the fold at the base and secure with string.

To prepare the oven for a soufflé
Move top shelf to center of oven and preheat to required temperature (375°F). If the temperature is too low the soufflé texture will be dry like sponge cake. It should be well risen, the top golden and firm to the touch but the center still soft and creamy.

Points to watch
1. The basis of a hot soufflé is a butter and flour roux made into a thick sauce with milk, coffee, fruit juice or purée, into which the egg yolks are beaten. Cool slightly before adding yolks or they will curdle.
2. Do not try to fold the beaten egg whites into the sauce in a small saucepan. Pour the sauce over the egg whites in a large bowl, about a third at a time; fold and cut it in lightly and quickly.
3. Do not remove paper collar until serving as a cold draft can collapse the soufflé in minutes.

Steamed apricot soufflé

1½ cups apricot purée (see page 57)
3 tablespoons butter
4 tablespoons flour
Sugar to taste
3 egg yolks, beaten
1 tablespoon lemon juice
3–4 egg whites
2 tablespoons slivered almonds
Apricot sauce (see page 28)

Cooking Time: 1 hour
Oven: 375°F

Stewed fresh, dried or canned fruit can be used for this recipe. Strain and purée the fruit, measure and make up to 1¼ cups with the liquid. Use the surplus liquid for the sauce. The amount of sugar to use in the soufflé mixture will depend on the original sweetness of the purée. Greengages, plums, raspberries, loganberries or blackberries can replace the apricots.

Prepare a 6 inch soufflé dish and the oven (see page 62). Melt butter in a small saucepan, remove from heat and blend in flour. Stir in the apricot purée, bring to the simmer and cook, stirring for 3–5 minutes. Sweeten to taste. Cool slightly and gradually beat in egg yolks. Add lemon juice. Beat egg whites until stiff but not dry and fold into mixture. Pour into prepared soufflé dish and stand it in a roasting pan with sufficient cold water to come halfway up. Bake for 1 hour, or until set and springy to the touch.

Meanwhile toast slivered almonds under the broiler and make the sauce. When the soufflé is ready, brush the top with a little of the sauce and sprinkle on the almonds. Serve immediately, with the sauce separately.

Cold sweet soufflés

Cold soufflé is made quite differently from hot soufflé, with a custard base into which whipped cream and beaten egg whites are folded. It is not baked, but set with gelatin. The setting mixture is poured into a soufflé dish with a paper collar like a hot soufflé (see page 62) so that it stands 3 inches above the top of the dish. It makes an impressive and delicious cold dessert for parties with no risk of collapse.

Points to watch

1. Take care to dissolve the gelatin completely before adding it to the basic mixture as it will not melt later but leave little nodules in the finished soufflé, which also may not set owing to insufficient melted gelatin.
2. Do not over-whip the egg whites. They must be stiff, but if they are too dry and brittle it will be difficult to fold them in smoothly.
3. Do not be tempted to fold the beaten egg whites into the setting mixture until it is thick and heavy, or it will separate as it sets into a jelly in the base of the dish with foam on top. If the mixture is slightly too set, beat again before folding in the cream and egg whites.

Steamed apricot soufflé; Preparing a soufflé dish

Fresh orange and lemon soufflé

3 eggs, separated
¾ cup sugar
½ cup orange juice
¼ cup lemon juice
½ oz (2 envelopes) powdered gelatin
1½ cups heavy cream
2 tablespoons Orange
Curaçao, Cointreau or Grand Marnier
(optional)

To decorate:
Crystallized orange and lemon slices
Pistachio nuts or angelica
Heavy cream (optional)

This is a light, refreshing dessert to follow a rich main course. The proportion of orange to lemon juice can be varied to taste. Orange juice by itself tends to be insipid and needs sharpening with lemon or grapefruit.

Prepare a 6 inch soufflé dish (see page 62). Beat the egg yolks, sugar and fruit in a large bowl over a saucepan of boiling water (take care the water does not touch the bowl), until the mixture is thick and foamy and falls from the beater in ribbons which hold their shape for a few seconds before sinking back into the mixture. Remove from heat. Dissolve the gelatin in a cup with 3–4 tablespoons of the boiling water from the pan. When thoroughly dissolved, beat into the fruit mixture. Set aside to chill and thicken. Beat the egg whites until stiff but not brittle. Whip the cream to a soft peak. When the fruit mixture has thickened and is beginning to set, fold in the cream and then the egg whites. Fold in the liqueur last. Turn the mixture into the soufflé dish, smooth the top and refrigerate until set. Peel off the paper collar with the help of a knife dipped in hot water. Cut the orange and lemon slices into small wedges, halve or chop the pistachio nuts (or angelica) and decorate to taste, with whipped cream if using. Stand the soufflé dish on a dessert plate to serve.

Coffee praline soufflé

For the praline:
¼ cup sugar
⅓ cup unblanched almonds

For the soufflé:
3 eggs, separated
Scant ½ cup sugar
2 tablespoons instant coffee powder
¾ cup boiling water
½ oz (2 envelopes) powdered gelatin
3 tablespoons cold water
1¼ cups heavy cream
2 tablespoons Tia Maria (optional)

Prepare a 6 inch soufflé dish. First make the praline so that it has time to cool. Put the sugar and almonds into a small thick saucepan over gentle heat. When the sugar is dissolved, stir carefully to coat the almonds and continue cooking until rich golden brown and smelling of toffee. Pour onto an oiled baking sheet, spreading it out. When cold and brittle, remove and chop small or grind in a mill, but not to fine powder.

Mix the egg yolks and sugar in a large bowl. Dissolve the coffee in the boiling water and add gradually. Whisk over a saucepan of boiling water until thick and foamy. Remove from heat and continue beating until cold. Soak the gelatin in the cold water, dissolve over gentle heat and stir into the soufflé mixture. Place in a bowl of cold water with ice and stir gently from time to time until beginning to set.

Meanwhile beat egg whites until stiff but not dry. Whip cream into soft peaks and fold about two-thirds into the coffee mixture. Fold in egg whites and half the praline. Mix in the Tia Maria if using. Turn into the soufflé dish, smooth top and chill. When set, peel off paper collar with the help of a knife dipped in hot water. Coat the sides of the soufflé with some of the remaining praline. Whip remaining cream stiff enough to pipe and decorate the top of the soufflé. Garnish with the rest of the praline.

Coffee praline soufflé; Fresh orange and lemon soufflé

Variations

Raspberry, loganberry or apricot soufflé
Follow the recipe for Orange and Lemon Soufflé and use a purée of fresh, frozen or canned fruit instead of the juice. If using canned fruit, strain off the juice, then purée the fruit, measure and make up to ¾ cup with juice. This gives you a good thick purée.
Sharpen the soufflé mixture with lemon juice to taste just before folding in the egg whites. If adding liqueurs Kirsch is a good choice with Raspberry and Loganberry Soufflé; apricot brandy with the Apricot.

Fresh tangerine soufflé
Follow the recipe for Orange and Lemon Soufflé, using tangerine instead of orange juice. Kirsch or the orange based liqueurs are suitable for flavoring. Decorate with tangerine segments, or the rind blanched in boiling water and cut into an attractive design.

Fresh grapefruit soufflé
Follow the recipe for Orange and Lemon Soufflé using ½ cup grapefruit juice and ¼ cup orange juice instead of lemon.

Honey and lemon cream mold

2 large eggs, separated
2 tablespoons honey, warmed
*Finely grated rind and juice of 1
lemon*
2½ cups half-and-half
½ oz (2 envelopes) powdered gelatin
2 tablespoons hot water

Beat the egg yolks and honey together until creamy. Add lemon rind to the half-and-half and heat slowly in a thick saucepan without boiling. Whisk a little hot half-and-half into the egg yolk mixture and blend this into the hot half-and-half. Stir over gentle heat until the custard clings to the back of the wooden spoon. Strain into a cold bowl and cool. Dissolve gelatin thoroughly in the hot water and stir into the custard with the lemon juice. Beat the egg whites until stiff but not brittle and fold into the custard. Reheat until nearly boiling. Rinse a 4 cup mold with cold water, pour in mixture slowly, cool and then refrigerate until set. It will separate as it sets into a fluffy top and lemon gelatin base which will be reversed when it is unmolded. Serve with fruit compote or fresh summer fruit, and plain whipped cream.

Fresh apricot mold

1 cup sugar
2½ cups water
1 thin piece lemon peel
1 lb fresh apricots
½ oz (2 envelopes) powdered gelatin
3 tablespoons hot water

To serve:
Crumbled meringues
or ratafias
Heavy cream or light cream

A gelatin mold is a fine way to use apricots, plums, or peaches which are slightly underripe. Dissolve the sugar in the water. Add the lemon rind and boil for 5 minutes. Add the apricots and cook gently for 10–15 minutes; do not overcook. Lift the fruit out with a draining spoon onto a plate. Remove skins, put these back in the simmering syrup and continue cooking to reduce slightly.
Meanwhile halve and pit the apricots and put them in a glass serving bowl, or divide between individual dishes. Strain and measure off 2½ cups of apricot syrup. Dissolve the gelatin in the hot water and stir into the syrup. Pour over the fruit and leave in a cool place to set. Serve decorated with whipped cream and crumbled meringues or accompany with a jug of cream.

Fruit Chartreuse

1½ 3 oz packages lemon-flavored Jell-O
11 oz can mandarins
8 oz cherries or grapes
4 ripe bananas
Juice of 1 lemon

To decorate:
Heavy cream

This colorful dessert is not so difficult to make as it looks. The secret is patience – set one layer at a time or the fruit will swim about and lose its pattern. Choose any fruits of contrasting color.
Dissolve the Jell-O in 1¼ cups boiling water. Add the drained mandarin juice and sufficient cold water to make liquid up to 2½ cups. Pit cherries or seed grapes. Peel bananas and cut each across into 3 equal pieces. Brush with lemon juice to prevent discoloration.
Rinse out a shallow 4 cup mold with cold water. Pour a thin layer of the dissolved Jell-O over the base and refrigerate until set. When firm arrange mandarin sections and cherries or grapes in an attractive pattern on it, dipping each piece in liquid Jell-O first. Chill until firm, then cover with a layer of Jell-O and chill. When set, stand banana sticks round sides of mold, dipping each piece in liquid Jell-O. Fill center with mixed fruit, cover with more Jell-O to fill mold and refrigerate. To serve, unmold and decorate with piped whipped cream and any remaining fruit.

Fresh apricot mold; Fruit chartreuse; Honey and lemon cream mold

Chocolate cream ice

2 oz semi-sweet chocolate
2½ cups light cream
Scant ½ cup sugar
3 egg yolks, beaten
2–3 tablespoons Marsala or sweet
sherry

To decorate:
Heavy cream
Crystallized violets
Pistachio nuts or walnuts

This ice cream made with a chocolate custard base can be varied by flavoring it with instant coffee or rum, or given a crunchy texture by folding in 2–3 tablespoons of praline (see page 66) with the egg whites.

Break up chocolate and melt in a bowl over hot water. Put the cream over gentle heat. Add a little hot cream to the melted chocolate, stir until smooth and blend back into cream with the sugar. Add 2–3 tablespoons of the chocolate mixture to the egg yolks and stir this mixture back into the pan. Continue to stir over gentle heat (in a double boiler if preferred) until cream thickens into a thin custard and coats the back of the wooden spoon. Do not boil or it will separate.

Cool, stirring occasionally to prevent a skin forming, then add Marsala or sherry. Pour into freezing tray or molds and freeze until stiff. Serve decorated with whipped cream, crystallized violets and chopped nuts.

Slimline orange sherbet

1 6 oz container frozen, or ¾ cup fresh orange juice
1 large orange
1¼ cups plain yogurt
½ oz (2 envelopes) powdered gelatin
¼ cup hot water
2 egg whites

To garnish:
Fresh mint

A refreshing water ice made without sugar, this will have special appeal for calorie-counting guests.

Defrost the frozen orange juice. Grate the rind finely off the orange and add to the juice. Mix into the yogurt. Dissolve the gelatin in hot water, blend with the mixture and leave to thicken. Beat the egg whites to a stiff snow and when the yogurt begins to set, fold in carefully. Pour the sherbet mixture into a freezer container and freeze.

Peel the pith off the orange. Take a sharp knife and cut down to the center of the orange on either side of each section and lift it out from between the dividing membranes.

To serve fill individual glasses with spoonfuls of frozen sherbet interspersed with orange sections. Garnish with sprigs of fresh mint.

Brown bread ice cream

1¼ cups wholewheat breadcrumbs
½ cup sugar
¾ cup heavy cream
½ cup light cream
Generous ¾ cup confectioners' sugar, sifted
1 egg, separated
2 tablespoons rum or Marsala

To decorate:
½ cup crushed peanut brittle or praline (see page 66)
Heavy cream (optional)

A modern version of a popular Victorian ice cream which may sound a little dull but tastes delicious.

Spread the crumbs on a baking sheet and sprinkle with the sugar. Bake in a moderately hot oven until crisp and golden, shaking the tray from time to time. Spread on a cold plate to cool.

Beat the creams together, gradually adding the confectioners' sugar. Beat the egg yolk with the rum or Marsala and beat into the cream.

Beat the egg white until stiff but not brittle and fold into the mixture with the breadcrumbs. Turn into a 2½ cup mold, cover tightly with foil and freeze. To unmold dip briskly into hot water and turn out. Decorate with crushed peanut brittle or praline and serve with butterscotch or chocolate sauce. Alternatively serve in individual glasses, pour over the sauce, top with whipped cream and nut brittle.

Brown bread ice cream; Chocolate cream ice; Iced plum pudding; Slimline orange sherbet

Iced plum pudding

1¼ cups heavy cream
1 cup condensed milk
1 teaspoon ground allspice
½ teaspoon grated nutmeg
4 teaspoons instant coffee powder
¼ cup chopped citron peel
⅓ cup chopped walnuts
¾ cup dark raisins
¾ cup golden raisins
¾ cup glacé cherries, chopped
Finely grated rind of 1 orange
½ teaspoon vanilla extract
2–3 tablespoons rum or brown sherry

To decorate:
Heavy cream
Glacé cherries, halved

This is a recipe from Australia where Christmas falls in the hottest days of summer and hot Christmas pudding may not be too welcome.

Beat half of the cream together with the condensed milk, spices and coffee. Pour into a refrigerator tray and freeze until stiffened. Turn into a bowl and again beat until light and creamy. Whip remaining cream to soft peak and fold into the mixture with the fruit, nuts and orange rind. Flavor to taste with vanilla and rum or sherry. Pour into a pudding mold and freeze hard.

Move mold from freezer to refrigerator about 1 hour before required. To serve, dip mold quickly into hot water and unmold onto a serving platter. Pipe whipped cream around edges and decorate with cherries.

Iced raspberry parfait

1 lb fresh raspberries (approx. 3 cups)
2 egg whites
½ cup sugar
¼ cup water
2 tablespoons lemon juice
1¼ cups heavy cream

To finish:
Heavy cream
Whole raspberries or crystallized rose petals

Especially delicious made with fresh raspberries, loganberries, strawberries or apricots, this is also very good made with any canned fruit except strawberries.

Sieve the raspberries. If using canned fruit strain off the juice, sieve the fruit, measure the purée and make up to 1¼ cups with some of the juice. Beat the egg whites until stiff.

Put the sugar and water in a small saucepan and place over gentle heat. Stir until sugar has dissolved, then bring to the boil and cook rapidly without stirring until the syrup will form a thread (250°F). Allow the syrup to stop bubbling, then pour slowly onto the beaten egg whites in a thin steady stream, holding the saucepan well above the bowl and stirring continuously with a wooden spoon. When all the sugar is in, continue to beat until the mixture is thick and shiny and forms soft peaks. Stir in the fruit purée and lemon juice. Whip the cream into soft peaks and gradually fold in the fruit mixture. Sharpen to taste with lemon juice.

Pour into a mold or individual molds and freeze. Transfer Parfait from freezer to the refrigerator 1 hour before serving. Dip the mold briefly in hot water to unmold. Decorate with whipped cream and whole raspberries or crystallized rose petals. Serve with wafer cookies or plain petits fours.

Iced melon sherbet

1 small honeydew melon
½ cup sugar
1 lemon
1 egg white

To decorate:
⅔ cup heavy cream
4 Maraschino or glacé cherries
8 fresh mint leaves or angelica diamonds

This is an ideally refreshing dessert to serve after a rich or highly-spiced main course, such as curry. It is a charming decorative sweet for a dinner party.

Cut the melon in half lengthwise, discard the seeds and scoop out the flesh. Put this in a blender with the sugar and 2 tablespoons of lemon juice. Blend until the sugar is dissolved. Pour into a freezer container and freeze until mushy.

Meanwhile cut the two pieces of melon shell in half lengthwise. Reform each into original shape, using two bowls of matching size lined with foil. Chill in refrigerator.

When the melon mixture is mushy turn into a bowl and whisk. Beat egg white until stiff and fold into melon mixture; sharpen to taste with lemon juice. Pour into two melon shells, cover with foil and freeze. About 1 hour before required, separate into four sections using a knife dipped into hot water. Place wedges on four dessert plates. Using a rose nozzle, pipe a zig-zag of whipped cream along the top of each wedge. Place a cherry in the center with a frosted mint or angelica leaf on either side. Return to refrigerator until serving.

If you cannot get a small melon for 4 servings, use half a large one and cut it into 4 wedges.

Chocolate ripple pears

¼ lb semi-sweet chocolate
3 tablespoons golden or light corn
syrup
½ cup light cream
4 ripe dessert pears
Vanilla and chocolate ice cream
Macaroons or ratafia biscuits

For maximum effect pour the rich chocolate sauce hot over the ice cream and pears. But the sauce is also very good cold, and freezes well.

First make the chocolate cream sauce. Break up the chocolate and melt in a bowl over hot water. Blend in golden syrup. Heat the cream, without boiling, and gradually stir into the chocolate mixture. Keep warm over the hot water. (If serving cold, remove from heat and stir occasionally until chilled.)

Core, halve and peel the pears. Put two scoops of vanilla and chocolate ice cream in each dessert dish and arrange a half pear on either side. Pour over the hot chocolate cream sauce and garnish with macaroons or ratafia biscuits, either whole or crushed.

Fire and ice

4 medium cooking apples
2 tablespoons butter or margarine
¼ cup dark brown sugar
About ½ cup cider or water
Vanilla ice cream
4 shelled walnuts or crushed ginger nuts

Cooking Time: 30–40 minutes
Oven: 375°F

The contrast of hot sharp-tasting roast apple with an ice cold sweet topping makes exciting eating.

Wipe and core the apples. With a sharp knife, slit the skin round the "equator". Place the apples in a well-buttered fireproof dish and fill their centers with brown sugar. Add sufficient cider or water to cover base of baking dish. Cover with a buttered sheet of wax paper or foil. Bake in a preheated moderately hot oven for 30 minutes until tender – test with a skewer and do not overcook. Remove from oven, lift skin carefully off the apples and place in individual dishes.

Keep the apples warm while you boil the liquid in the base of the dish briskly until reduced to a syrupy consistency. Pour over the apples. Top each apple with a generous helping of ice cream and a shelled walnut or crushed ginger nut. Serve immediately.

Pineapple igloos

3 egg whites
¾ cup sugar
4 pineapple slices
1 pint strawberry ice cream

To garnish:
Glacé cherries
Angelica leaves
Superfine sugar

Cooking Time: 4–5 minutes
Oven: 450°F

This is a version of Baked Alaska made in individual portions with pineapple instead of sponge cake for the base. Use bought ice cream or the Strawberry Parfait (see page 72).

Preheat the oven and place a shelf near the top. Beat the egg whites until very stiff and dry. Sift in ¼ cup sugar and continue beating until stiff and shiny. Fold in the remaining sugar.

Place the pineapple slices on 4 ovenproof glass dishes. Pile the ice cream evenly on top so that it does not project over the edge. Swirl the meringue over each one, covering the ice cream and pineapple completely. Be careful to seal the edges right onto the plates or the ice cream will melt and leak.

Decorate with glacé cherries and angelica and dust with superfine sugar. Put the dishes on a baking sheet and bake on top shelf of the preheated oven for 4–5 minutes, until delicately colored and crisp. Serve at once.

Fire and ice; Chocolate ripple pears; Pineapple igloos

Apricot rum baba

Apricot rum baba

$\frac{3}{4}$ *cup flour*
$\frac{1}{4}$ *teaspoon salt*
$\frac{1}{4}$ *oz fresh yeast; or* $1\frac{1}{2}$ *teaspoons active dry yeast*
2 tablespoons sugar
$\frac{1}{4}$ *cup warm milk*
2 eggs, beaten
5 tablespoons butter, creamed

For the rum syrup:
$\frac{1}{2}$ *cup sugar*
$\frac{3}{4}$ *cup water*
$\frac{1}{2}$ *cup rum*

For the decoration and filling:
Apricot glaze (see page 88)
$\frac{1}{2}$ *lb apricots, fresh or canned*
Angelica
$\frac{2}{3}$ *cup heavy cream*

Cooking Time: 40 minutes
Oven: 400°F, then reduce to 350°F

This is a lovely party sweet. In summer you can use strawberries, and Kirsch instead of rum in the syrup.

Sift flour and salt into a bowl and put to warm. Cream the yeast with the sugar, add the warm milk and beaten eggs. Gradually stir into the flour and beat to a smooth batter. Cover the bowl with a clean cloth and leave in a warm place to prove for about 45 minutes or until the dough has doubled in bulk. Beat in the butter gradually. Half fill a greased 7 inch Baba ring and leave in warm place until the dough rises to the rim.

Bake in a preheated moderately hot oven for 10 minutes, then reduce to moderate and continue cooking for 30 minutes or until a skewer inserted comes out clean. Remove from oven. Allow to shrink for 5–10 minutes, loosen with a knife and turn out onto a shallow pie dish, upside down.

Dissolve the sugar in the water, then boil fast until reduced to a syrup. Cool slightly and add the rum. Prick the Baba and spoon over the syrup. Baste frequently until all the syrup is absorbed.

Coat the Baba with Apricot Glaze. Arrange 8 apricot halves on the top and brush with glaze. Cut the angelica into leaves and insert between apricots. Cut up remaining apricots, fold into the whipped cream and pile into the center of the Baba.

Mandarin charlotte russe

Mandarin charlotte russe

11 oz can mandarin oranges
1½ 3 oz packages lemon-flavored Jell-O
½ oz angelica
18 ladyfingers
1¼ cups heavy cream
1–2 tablespoons Orange
Curaçao or Cointreau (optional)

You can make this sweet the day before the party. In summer fill it with fresh raspberries or strawberries.

Rinse a 2½ cup Charlotte mold with cold water. Drain the fruit. Dissolve the Jell-O thoroughly in 1¼ cups boiling water and add the fruit syrup making the liquid up to 2 cups plus 2 tablespoons with water if necessary.

Pour a thin layer of liquid Jell-O into the bottom of the mold and put in refrigerator to set.

Cut off one rounded end of the ladyfinger so they are ½ inch shorter than the sides of the mold.

When the first layer of Jell-O is set, arrange some of the mandarin sections on it in an attractive pattern with angelica diamonds, dipping each piece in the liquid Jell-O before you put it in place. Refrigerate until set. When the pattern is firm cover with another layer of Jell-O and refrigerate. Meanwhile whip the cream until fairly stiff and fold in the liqueur if using.

When the Jell-O in the mold is firm dip the sugared side of the cookies one at a time in liquid Jell-O and stand them closely together all round the sides of the mold, sugar side out. Fill the center with alternate layers of cream and mandarin sections, ending with cream.

Slowly spoon remaining Jell-O down sides of mold between the cookies, which will gradually absorb it. When Jell-O shows at the rim of the mold, chill Charlotte until required. Unmold and decorate with remaining cream and extra fruit if desired.

Summer rose meringue

For the Swiss Meringue:
1¾ cups confectioners' sugar, sifted
4 egg whites
¼ teaspoon vanilla extract

For the filling:
⅔ cup heavy cream
1–2 tablespoons Kirsch or sherry
2 teaspoons sugar
1½–2 cups loganberries, raspberries or strawberries
½ oz crystallized rose petals

Cooking Time: 80 minutes
Oven: 275°F

One of the advantages of this pretty dessert is that you can make the meringue baskets when convenient and store them in an airtight container or in the freezer until required. It takes only a few minutes to fill them so they are very practical for a buffet party; wild strawberries would make them a super treat. The recipe makes 6.

Put the egg whites and confectioners' sugar in a bowl over a saucepan of simmering water and follow the recipe for Swiss Meringue (page 89). Flavor with vanilla extract. Line 2 baking sheets with non-stick parchment or wax paper and draw 18 3 inch circles. If using wax paper, oil lightly. Put the meringue mixture in a pastry bag with a large rose nozzle. Pipe rings just inside the circles. Fill in 6 rings with more meringue to make flat discs. Bake in preheated slow oven for 45 minutes or until crisp and delicately colored. Remove from oven, cool and loosen meringue.

Mount 2 meringue rings on each disc, sticking them together with remaining meringue mixture. Return to oven for 20 minutes until firm. Remove and cool. Whip cream until stiff, fold in Kirsch or sherry and sugar to taste. Fold in prepared berries, pile into baskets and decorate with crystallized rose petals. For buffets serve baskets in paper meringue cases.

Pavlova cake

For the meringue:
3 egg whites
¾ cup superfine sugar
1 teaspoon cornstarch
¼ teaspoon vanilla extract
1 teaspoon lemon juice

For the filling:
1¼ cups heavy cream
1 cup hulled strawberries or raspberries
¼ lb cherries, pitted
4 ripe apricots or greengages, halved
2 ripe peaches, sliced

To decorate:
¼ lb redcurrants
1 egg white
2 tablespoons superfine sugar

Cooking Time: 1¼–1½ hours
Oven: 300°F

This Australian sweet, named for the famous ballerina, is topped with passion fruit in its country of origin.

Draw a 7 inch circle of non-stick parchment or lightly-oiled wax paper and place on a baking sheet. Beat the egg whites until very stiff and dry. Strain and beat in half the sugar and continue beating until the mixture is stiff and shiny. Strain the remaining sugar with the cornstarch and fold into the mixture with the vanilla extract and lemon juice.

Spread the meringue on the circle and build up into a bowl-shaped shell, swirling the meringue round the outside of the shell. Bake in the center of a slow oven for 1¼–1½ hours until firm and delicately colored. Allow to cool before removing parchment or paper. The shell can be prepared in advance and stored in an airtight container until required.

Wash and dry the redcurrants. Beat the egg white until liquid. Dip little bunches of the redcurrants into this and then into the sugar. Chill in the refrigerator to crystallize.

Whip the cream and set 2 tablespoons aside for the topping with some of the prepared fruit. Fold the rest of the fruit carefully into the cream and pile in the center of the meringue. Top with the remaining fruit, swirl the rest of the cream in the center and decorate with the crystallized redcurrants.

Summer rose meringue; Pavlova cake

Strawberry meringue flan

Strawberry meringue flan

2 egg whites
Rounded ½ cup sugar
1 cup heavy cream
1 lb strawberries

Cooking Time: 1 hour
Oven: 275°F

Line a baking sheet with non-stick parchment or wax paper. Draw two 7 inch circles in pencil. Lightly oil the wax paper.

Whisk the egg whites until very stiff and dry. Sift in 2 tablespoons of sugar and whisk again until very stiff and shiny. Sift and fold in the remaining sugar quickly and lightly. Do not over-fold or the meringue will fall. Fill the meringue mixture into a large pastry bag with a large rose nozzle.

Pipe a ring of meringue round one circle just inside the pencil mark. Pipe 8 small rosettes round about with a base the same width as the piped ring. Pipe remaining meringue mixture into the other circle and spread it out evenly into a flat disc.

Bake in preheated slow oven for about 1 hour until crisp. Remove from oven, lift off rosettes. Turn paper upside down on the table and peel the paper off the meringue ring and disc. If you lift meringues off the paper they may break.

Shortly before serving whip the cream and pipe a ring round the edge of the flat disc. Place meringue ring on top and press down gently. Pipe cream on the bottom of rosettes and press them on top of the ring. Halve the strawberries and arrange them neatly in meringue case. Decorate with remaining cream.

Hazelnut galette

Hazlenut galette

$\frac{1}{4}$ *lb hazelnuts*
1 cup flour
Pinch of salt
$\frac{1}{4}$ *cup sugar*
6 tablespoons butter

For the topping:
Scant $\frac{1}{2}$ cup sugar

For the filling:
1$\frac{1}{4}$ cups heavy cream
1 tablespoon sugar
4–5 fresh peaches

Cooking Time: 15–20 minutes
Oven: 350°F

Spread hazelnuts on a baking sheet. Toast under broiler, shaking frequently. Rub in a dry cloth to remove skins. Chop 1 oz roughly and grind the rest.
Sift the flour and salt into bowl and mix in the ground nuts and sugar. Rub in butter with finger tips until of breadcrumb consistency. Knead lightly and chill for 30 minutes or until dough is firm. Shape into a thick roll, divide into 4 and roll out into 4 thin circles.
Place the circles on a greased baking sheet and bake in a preheated moderate oven for 15–20 minutes until brown and set. Remove from oven and cool.
Put the sugar in a small thick saucepan over gentle heat and stir gently until dissolved. Increase heat and boil briskly without stirring until a rich caramel color.
Pour some over one cookie, spreading it evenly with an oiled knife. Sprinkle the roughly chopped nuts round the edge before the caramel sets.
Prepare the filling shortly before Galette is to be served. Whip cream and fold in sugar. Peel and slice the peaches. Arrange a few slices in the center of the caramelized cookie. Warm up remaining caramel and trickle it over them, pulling the caramel into strands like spun sugar. Spread the cream over the other cookies, cover with sliced peaches and pile the layers on top of each other with the decorated cookie on top.
Fresh raspberries make an excellent alternative.

Chocolate biscuit gâteau

Chocolate biscuit gâteau

8 oz semi-sweet chocolate
½ lb (2 sticks) butter
2 eggs, beaten
2 tablespoons sugar
½ lb graham crackers

To decorate:
½ cup heavy cream
Glacé cherries
Angelica
Walnut halves

Grease a 6 inch cake pan with a detachable base. Break up the chocolate and put it in a bowl over a saucepan of simmering water to melt. Melt the butter gently in another pan. Beat the eggs with the sugar in a bowl. Pour in the melted butter in a steady stream, beating continuously. Now blend in the melted chocolate. Break up the graham crackers into small pieces and fold them into the chocolate. Turn the mixture into the cake tin and chill overnight, in the refrigerator.

To serve stand the cake pan on a canister at least 2 inches smaller than the base of the pan. Push the pan carefully down onto the table, leaving the base with the cake on the canister. Slide it onto a serving plate and decorate with piped whipped cream, cherries, angelica and walnut halves.

Chocolate, rum and raisin cheesecake

Chocolate, rum and raisin cheesecake

5 oz graham crackers
6 tablespoons butter
¼ cup brown sugar

For the filling:
⅓ cup dark raisins
2 tablespoons rum
2 eggs, separated
¼ cup sugar
1 teaspoon instant coffee
5 tablespoons boiling water
½ oz (2 envelopes) powdered gelatin
2 oz semi-sweet chocolate
½ lb cream cheese
1 cup heavy cream
2 tablespoons milk

To decorate:
⅔ cup heavy cream
Chocolate flakes or crystallized flowers and leaves

Vary this by using sweet sherry instead of rum or omitting the raisins altogether and using a double quantity of chocolate.
Serves 6–8.
Soak the raisins in rum, preferably overnight. Crush the graham crackers between sheets of wax paper until fine. Melt the butter and stir in the crumbs and sugar. Stir over gentle heat until well blended and press into a greased 9 inch flan dish or pan with a loose base. Refrigerate to harden well.
Mix egg yolks, sugar and the coffee dissolved in 2 tablespoons of the boiling water in the top of a double saucepan or in a bowl. Place over boiling water and stir steadily until the mixture clings to the back of the wooden spoon.
Dissolve gelatin thoroughly in 3 tablespoons of boiling water, stir into the egg mixture and remove from heat. Melt the chocolate with a little water in a bowl over boiling water. Stir until smooth and blend into mixture.
Beat the cream cheese and when the chocolate mixture is cold, stir it gradually into the cream cheese. Whisk the cream with the milk to soft peaks and fold into the mixture. Whisk the egg whites until stiff but not brittle and fold into mixture. Stir in rum-soaked raisins. Pour into flan dish or pan and refrigerate until firmly set.
Decorate with piped whipped cream and chocolate flakes or crystallized flowers and leaves.

Syllabub; Marrons Mont Blanc

Syllabub

1 lemon
½ cup medium white wine
3–4 tablespoons sugar
1¼ cups heavy cream

To decorate:
*Chopped pistachio nuts or crushed
praline (see page 66)*

Light and quickly prepared, this dessert is for immediate serving,
or can be kept overnight in the refrigerator.
Grate the rind delicately off the lemon so there is no trace
of pith. Put it in a bowl with the strained lemon juice, wine
and 3 tablespoons sugar. (You can leave this mixture to infuse
if there is time.) Strain out the lemon rind just before using.
Gradually add the cream, beating steadily until the mixture
stands in peaks. Taste and add more sugar if desired; this will
depend on the wine you have used.
Pour the Syllabub into goblets or custard cups, swirling it up
the center, and chill thoroughly.
Decorate with chopped pistachio nuts or crushed praline and
serve with cookies.

Marrons Mont Blanc

4 tablespoons unsalted butter
2 tablespoons sugar
8 oz can purée of marrons glacés
1–2 tablespoons sherry
Lemon juice to taste
⅔ cup heavy cream

To decorate:
*Ratafia biscuits or
miniature meringues*

These little mounds of chestnut purée, topped with whipped
cream like the snow-capped mountain from which they take
their name, are one of the most delicious of all desserts.
Cream together the butter and sugar. Stir the chestnut purée
and add it gradually to the creamed mixture. Flavor to taste
with sherry and lemon juice, stirring it in gradually to avoid
curdling.
Pile the chestnut purée into the center of individual dessert
dishes. Whip the cream and swirl onto the top of each little
mound. Arrange ratafia biscuits or miniature meringues round
the base. Chill until required.

Jersey jumbles; Country jam pudding

Country jam pudding

$1\frac{1}{3}$ cups self-rising flour
3 tablespoons sugar
4 tablespoons butter or margarine
1 egg, beaten
3–4 tablespoons jam, lemon custard
or mincemeat
Superfine sugar for dusting

Cooking Time: 15–20 minutes
Oven: 400°F

A simple, quick pudding to make which can be eaten hot or cold and packs well for picnics.

Mix the flour and sugar together. Rub in the fat with the tips of the fingers until the consistency of breadcrumbs. Mix into a stiff dough with the egg and a little water. Knead lightly and divide in half. Roll out thinly into 2 rectangles of the same size. Place one on a greased baking sheet, prick and spread with preserve, leaving a margin round the edge. Brush the margin with water and place the second rectangle on top. Press the edges together and pinch with finger and thumb into flutes. Prick the top in a pattern with a fork. Bake in a preheated moderately hot oven for 15–20 minutes until risen and golden brown. Remove from oven, sprinkle with superfine sugar and cut into squares. Serve hot with custard sauce or cold with plain whipped cream.

Jersey jumbles

$\frac{3}{4}$ cup flour
Pinch of salt
1 teaspoon baking powder
Pinch of ground ginger
Pinch of ground nutmeg
2 tablespoons butter or margarine
2 tablespoons sugar
1 egg, beaten
Deep fat for frying
Superfine sugar for dusting
Honey or syrup

Sift the flour, salt, baking powder and spices into a bowl. Rub in the fat with the finger tips. Mix in the sugar. Stir in the egg, adding a little water if necessary; the dough should be fairly stiff. Roll out on a floured board until about $\frac{1}{2}$ inch thick. Cut into 3 inch rounds. With a smaller cutter, remove the centers to leave rings. Work up remaining dough, roll out and cut into strips 3 inches × 1 inch. Shape into twists.

Heat the fat to 375°F; test by dropping in a piece of dough which should rise at once and start to swell. Drain the jumbles on paper towels and dust with sugar. Serve with warmed honey or syrup.

85

Zabaglione

3 egg yolks
Scant ½ cup sugar
1 teaspoon finely grated lemon rind
⅔ cup medium white wine or Marsala

This delicious wine whip can be served hot or cold, either as a light dessert or as a sweet sauce with hot sponge puddings or fruit compotes.
Beat the egg yolks with the sugar and lemon rind until white, then beat in the wine. Place the bowl over a saucepan of simmering water and continue beating until the mixture thickens and falls in ribbons from the beater. Pour into large wineglasses and serve at once as the mixture is likely to fall. Serve with cookies.

Cold zabaglione

6 egg yolks
Scant ½ cup sugar
Finely grated rind of 1 orange
⅔ cup Marsala or white wine
¼ cup heavy cream
Chopped pistachio nuts or orange peel

Follow the method for making hot Zabaglione and when the mixture has thickened to ribbon consistency, remove from heat, place in a bowl of iced water and continue beating until cold. Very lightly whisk the cream with a fork and fold into the mixture. Pour into goblets and chill in refrigerator until required. Decorate with chopped pistachio nuts or fine twists of orange peel and serve with cookies. Alternatively pour over sliced fresh peaches, strawberries or fresh fruit salad.

Atholl brose

¼ cup medium oatmeal or ground almonds
3–4 tablespoons whisky
1 tablespoon lemon juice
2 tablespoons clear honey
⅔ cup heavy cream

To decorate:
Twists of fresh lemon

This version of Syllabub is much better made with toasted oatmeal rather than with ground almonds. The amount of honey can be adjusted to taste. Spread the oatmeal on a pan and toast for a few minutes under the broiler, shaking frequently so that it browns evenly. Leave to cool.
Mix together the whisky, lemon juice and honey. Gradually beat in the cream until the mixture stands in soft peaks. Fold in the toasted oatmeal and turn into goblets. Chill until required. Decorate each goblet with a lemon twist and serve with thin shortbread cookies.

Peppermint chocolate pears

10–12 mint chocolate creams
4 ripe Comice pears
2 oz crystallized ginger or glacé cherries, chopped
⅔ cup light cream
⅓ cup walnuts, chopped

This is a good party sweet for the youngsters and one they can easily make for themselves.
Cut up the chocolate mints and put them in a bowl over a saucepan of simmering water to melt.
Core pears from the bottom, leaving top with stalk intact. Peel and slice a sliver off the base so that pears will stand upright. Stuff with chopped ginger or cherries and place each pear in a small dessert dish.
Heat the cream, without boiling, and add to the peppermint cream. Stir until smooth and pour over the pears. Sprinkle with chopped walnuts and serve at once.

Zabaglione; Atholl brose; Cold zabaglione; Peppermint chocolate pears

Belgian fruit tart

8 in flan case of sweet shortcrust pastry
(see page 50)
Pâtisserie Cream, vanilla flavor (see
page 92)
¼ lb green or black grapes
2 large bananas
Juice of ½ lemon
Apricot Glaze

For the Apricot glaze:
⅓ cup apricot jam
1 tablespoon lemon juice

You can vary the filling for this tart by choosing any fresh or canned fruit available. Use a redcurrant glaze for red berries or cherries and golden apricot glaze for other fruit. Serve the tart the day it is filled or the pastry will lose its crispness, but the flan case can be baked in advance and stored in a tin.

First make the vanilla-flavored Pâtisserie Cream and leave it to cool, stirring continuously to prevent a skin forming. Meanwhile slit the grapes down one side and remove the pits. Peel and slice the bananas and pour over the lemon juice to prevent discoloration.

When the Pâtisserie Cream is cold spread it in the flan case. Arrange the fruit on top in an attractive pattern. Make the Apricot Glaze by dissolving apricot jam with a little lemon juice over a low heat. Spoon carefully over the fruit. To give the tart a professional finish brush the glaze over the top edges of the pastry.

Variation

Raspberry, strawberry or cherry tart
Prepare 1 pound of fresh raspberries, hulled strawberries or pitted cherries. Flavor the Pâtisserie Cream with lemon juice and coat with Redcurrant Glaze.

Swiss raspberry charlotte

15 oz can raspberries
1 tablespoon cornstarch
1 egg yolk, beaten
½ cup light cream
1–2 tablespoons lemon juice
Sugar to taste
18 ladyfingers

For the Swiss meringue:
1–2 egg whites
2 tablespoons fruit syrup
¾ cup confectioners' sugar, sifted

Cooking Time: 20–25 minutes
Oven: 300°F

Strain the juice off the fruit, measure and add water to make up to 1 cup. Put cornstarch in a small saucepan, blend with a little juice into a smooth paste and then stir in remaining juice. Heat, stirring steadily with a wooden spoon, and simmer for 3–5 minutes until thickened and clear. Remove from heat. Mix the egg yolk and cream together and stir gradually into the sauce. Add lemon juice and sugar to taste.

Cut one rounded end from each ladyfinger. Pour a thin layer of raspberry cream in the bottom of a 6 inch soufflé dish and stand the ladyfingers round the dish. Fill with layers of fruit and cream. Cover the cream with a layer of drained fruit, then another layer of cream, a layer of fruit and cover with the remaining cream.

To make the Swiss Meringue put one egg white, fruit syrup and confectioners' sugar (or 2 egg whites and confectioners' sugar) in a bowl over a saucepan of simmering water. Beat together until thick and making soft peaks. Remove from heat and beat until cool. Flavor to taste with lemon, vanilla or fruit juice.

Pipe the meringue onto the Charlotte, covering the filling and rising pyramid style in the center. Bake in a moderate oven for 20 minutes or until the meringue is delicately colored. Serve cold.

Strawberry tart; Belgian fruit tart
Swiss raspberry charlotte

Portuguese walnut pudding

Portuguese walnut pudding

1½ cups broken walnuts
¼ teaspoon ground allspice
4 eggs, separated
1 cup sugar
½ cup walnut halves
2 tablespoons butter
1 tablespoon Kirsch

Cooking Time: 1½ hours

The Portuguese, like the English, are very fond of puddings. This one is made with walnuts and much enjoyed in both countries.

Grind the broken walnuts or chop finely and mix with the spice. Beat the egg yolks and sugar together until pale and creamy. Beat the egg whites until stiff but not brittle and fold into the egg yolk mixture alternately with the ground walnuts.

Turn into a buttered 3 cup mold, leaving room for the pudding to rise, and cover with greased foil. Steam for 1½ hours (see page 10) until set and springy to the touch; or test with a skewer. Allow to shrink slightly before unmolding onto a serving dish. Meanwhile fry the walnut halves in the butter until slightly crisp, then add the Kirsch.

Serve hot, garnished with the fried walnuts and accompanied by a bowl of Sherry Foam Sauce (see page 26); or cold, decorated with plain whipped cream and walnuts.

Bavarian prune and apricot torte; Italian frangipane flan

Italian frangipane flan

*8 in flan case of sweet shortcrust pastry
(page 50)
5 tablespoons unsalted butter
5 tablespoons flour
1 whole egg plus one yolk
2 tablespoons sugar
⅔ cup milk
2 teaspoons finely grated lemon rind
A few Ratafias or macaroons
1 tablespoon rum
¼ teaspoon vanilla extract
Raspberry jam*

Melt 3 tablespoons of the butter in a small saucepan. Remove from heat and blend in the flour. Beat the eggs and stir in gradually. Add the sugar and blend in the milk. Replace the pan on the burner and heat gently, stirring continuously until the mixture thickens and begins to leave the sides of the pan. Remove from heat and stir in the grated lemon rind, crushed ratafias, rum and vanilla extract. Heat the remaining butter in a small pan until it turns nut brown, then stir it into the cream mixture to give it the characteristic frangipane flavor. Spread the bottom of the flan case with jam. Pour in the frangipane cream and smooth the top.
When cold decorate with rosettes of piped plain whipped cream and halved or chopped pistachio kernels.

Bavarian prune and apricot torte

*2 cups flour
¼ lb (1 stick) plus 1 tablespoon unsalted butter
½ cup sugar
3 egg yolks, beaten
¼ teaspoon vanilla extract
Scant ½ cup water*

*For the topping:
½ cup prunes, soaked
⅓ cup apricots, soaked
2–3 tablespoons lemon juice
Superfine sugar for dusting*

Cooking Time: 25 minutes
Oven: 400°F, then reduce to 350°F

Sift the flour and rub in the butter with finger tips. Mix in the sugar. Beat egg yolks with vanilla extract and water and stir into dry ingredients. Add a little water if necessary to give a soft dough. Knead lightly on a floured board; pat out into a circle ¼ inch thick and place in a greased 8 inch layer cake tin. Chill for 30 minutes. Pit prunes and arrange on top of the torte with the apricots. Sprinkle with lemon juice and superfine sugar. Bake in a preheated hot oven for 15 minutes, reduce heat and cook for 10 minutes or until golden and set. Serve hot or cold with plain whipped cream.

Gâteau St Honoré

For the choux pastry:
3 tablespoons butter or margarine
⅔ cup water
⅔ cup flour, sifted
2 eggs, beaten

For the gâteau:
Sweet shortcrust pastry
(see page 50)
Pâtisserie Cream (see below); or
Whipped Cream (see page 23)
Rum or vanilla extract to taste
Scant ½ cup sugar

To decorate:
Crystallized rose and violet petals

Cooking Time: 35 minutes
Oven: 425°F, then reduce to 375°F

In France this is often used as a birthday party cake. For children the candles can be inserted in the little choux puffs which are coated with caramel or chocolate glacé icing.

Melt the butter in the water, bring to the boil and toss in the flour. Beat until smooth over gentle heat until the dough leaves the sides of the pan. Cool and beat in the eggs very gradually, 1 tablespoon at a time. If you do this too quickly the dough will be too soft to pipe.

Roll out the sweet shortcrust into a round about 8 inches across. Place on a greased baking sheet and prick well. Dampen the outside edge of the round. With a pastry bag and a ½ inch plain nozzle pipe a ring of choux pastry on top of the damp edge.

Pipe the rest of the choux pastry in small 'buns' the same width as the ring, on another greased baking sheet. Place shortcrust base on a shelf near the top of preheated oven, with small puffs below it. Bake for 15 minutes and reduce heat, reverse baking trays. Cook for 20 minutes more. Remove from oven and cool pastry. Slit choux ring and puffs to allow steam to escape.

Flavor Pâtisserie Cream or Whipped Cream with rum or vanilla. When cold, fill puffs.

Heat the sugar in small thick saucepan over gentle heat until it turns golden. Dip base of puffs in caramel and fix on ring. Trickle remaining caramel on top of puffs and quickly decorate with crushed rose petals and violet petals alternately, before caramel sets. Pile remaining cream into center and decorate top.

Pâtisserie cream

2 egg yolks
1 egg white
¼ cup sugar
3 tablespoons flour, sifted
1¼ cups milk
¼ teaspoon vanilla extract

Alternative flavourings:
Lemon juice, sweet sherry, rum

Beat the eggs and sugar together until nearly white. Gradually stir in the flour and then the milk. Pour into a small saucepan and bring to the boil, simmering steadily. Simmer for 3–5 minutes; it will not curdle. Flavor to taste with vanilla, lemon, sherry or rum. Pour onto a cold plate to cool and stir occasionally to prevent a skin forming. Use as required.

Gâteau St. Honoré

Chocolate roulade

Chocolate roulade

6 eggs, separated
¼ teaspoon vanilla extract
1 cup sugar
Generous ⅔ cup cocoa

For the filling:
¼ lb semi-sweet chocolate
2 tablespoons water
2 cups Whipped Cream (see page 23);
or heavy cream, whipped

To decorate:
⅔ cup heavy cream
Crystallized violets or lilac
Mint leaves or angelica diamonds

Cooking Time: 20 minutes
Oven: 350°F

This is a luscious party pudding from France.
Line a 13 × 8½ inch jelly roll tin with greased wax paper (see page 30).
Whip egg yolks, vanilla extract and sugar until creamy. Sift and fold in cocoa. Beat egg whites until stiff but not brittle and fold into mixture. Pour into prepared tin and spread evenly into corners.
Bake in preheated oven for 20 minutes or until set and springy to the touch, but still soft. Do not overcook or it will crack when rolled up. Remove from oven, allow to shrink slightly and turn out upside down on greased wax paper.
Break up chocolate and melt with the water in a bowl over a saucepan of simmering water. Stir until smooth and spread over cake. Cover with Whipped Cream (see page 23) or plain whipped cream. Roll up like Jelly Roll (see page 31). Remove to a serving platter and decorate with ribbons of piped whipped cream, crystallized flowers and mint leaves, angelica or nuts.
(Serves 8)

Glossary

ANGELICA: Herb with delicate muscatel flavor. Crystallized stems used to decorate cakes and desserts, or chopped and mixed with cake and pudding fruits.

BAIN MARIE: (French) a) Saucepan or baking dish standing in a large pan of simmering water either in oven or on hot plate. b) Double saucepan with water in lower container. A method of cooking or keeping food warm when it is liable to curdle if cooked quickly.

BAKING PARCHMENT: Silicone-treated lining material for baking pans which is non-stick and does not require greasing.

BAKING POWDER: Raising agent for flour consisting of 1 part cream of tartar to 2 parts baking soda. When liquid is added a gas is released and forms bubbles which raise the dough during cooking.

BAKING SODA: A raising agent used for soda bread and sour milk scones, moist gingerbreads etc.

BATTER: Mixture of flour, egg and milk or water used for coating food before frying or for making puddings and cakes which are fried or baked.

BLANCH: To scald fruit, almonds etc., in boiling water from 1–4 minutes so their skins can easily be removed.

CANDIED PEEL: Peel and pith of citrus fruits, usually orange, lemon and citron, cooked, boiled in syrup and dried. Used chopped in cakes and puddings.

CARAMELIZE: To boil sugar slowly until it turns into toffee consistency and becomes deep golden brown. Used for coloring, flavoring and glazing.

CANTALOUPE MELON: Round Musk Melon with rough skin and sweet orange-tinted flesh. Originally came from Cantaloupe, Italy.

CHAFING DISH: Frying pan used over a table burner, usually a spirit lamp, for flamed desserts and quickly cooked dishes.

CINNAMON: Aromatic bark of a tropical tree sold in sticks or ground. Used chiefly to spice cakes and puddings.

CITRON: Large lemon-shaped citrus fruit with very thick rind which has a fragrant flavor when crystallized and is used in cakes and puddings.

CLARIFIED BUTTER: Purified butter which has been heated and all suspended matter strained out, leaving pure fat for frying.

CREAM: (Fresh) Fat allowed to ride to top of milk and separated. Light Cream: 18–25% butterfat, will not whip. Heavy Cream: 36–40% butterfat, will whip, excellent for cold soufflés and pastry fillings.

COINTREAU: Orange-flavored liqueur.

COMPOTE: Fresh or diced fruit cooked in syrup.

CONDENSED MILK: Milk evaporated to thick viscous consistency, heavily sweetened and canned.

CURRANTS: (dried) Small Corinth grapes grown for drying.

DREDGE: To coat food with flour.

DUST: To coat food with sugar.

EVAPORATED MILK: Canned milk evaporated by two thirds, unsweetened.

FLAMBÉ: (French) Food flamed with alcohol such as brandy, rum or liqueur, during cooking or at the end and served while still flaming.

GALETTE: A thin flat cake, usually of pastry.

GATEAU: A cake made of rich sponge or pastry, usually with creamy filling, iced and decorated.

GLACÉ (French) Glazed with sugar syrup (fruit), or with confectioners' sugar (cakes).

GLAZE: A shiny coating made with jam, jelly or egg white and sugar for pastries, or with milk or egg yolk and water for breads.

GRAND MARNIER: Orange-flavored liqueur.

GRANULATED BROWN SUGAR: Honey-colored crystals of cane sugar.

GRIDDLE: A thick iron plate used on top of the stove for cooking scones, crêpes etc.

HARD SAUCE: Creamed butter and sugar flavored with brandy, rum or whisky and served chilled with hot puddings.

HONEYDEW MELON: Large oval melon, smooth skinned with sweet yellow/green flesh.

KIRSCH: White spirit distilled from wild black cherries.

LEMON CUSTARD: Preserve made with lemon juice, eggs, butter and sugar used as filling for cakes and pastries.

MANDARIN: Citrus fruit with loose skin similar to tangerine in shape and flavor.

MAPLE SYRUP: Sap from maple tree boiled into syrup and refined. Served with waffles and crêpes and various American sweets.

MARASCHINO: Liqueur made from wild cherries of Central Europe. "Maraschino cherries" are bottled and used for fillings, desserts, ice creams etc.

MOCHA: Coffee blended with chocolate for cakes, puddings and ice cream.

ORANGE CURAÇAO: Orange-flavored liqueur made from bitter oranges grown in Curaçao.

PASSION FRUIT: Tropical plum-sized fruit of the passion flower (granadillo) with wrinkled purple skin and fragrant juicy yellow pulp.

POTATO FLOUR: (Fécule) Finely milled potato starch used in delicate cakes and for thickening sauces.

PRALINE: Unblanched almonds cooked in caramelized sugar and crushed for serving with or garnishing cold desserts and cakes.

PURÉE: Raw or cooked fruit or other food, passed through a sieve or mashed in an electric blender.

RAISIN: Grapes, seeded or seedless, that have been sun dried.

RAMEKINS: Individual ovenproof dishes or cups.

RATAFIA BISCUITS: Tiny macaroons flavored with almonds, used crushed or whole.

ROUX: (French) Butter and flour, usually in equal quantities, cooked together and used as a base to thicken sauces.

SAGO: Starch made from the pith of the sago palm, used to make milk puddings or thicken sauces and purées.

SCALD: To heat milk or cream until just below boiling point. To plunge fruits briefly into boiling water to facilitate peeling.

SHERBET: (French) Water ice made with fruit juice.

SHORTENING: Animal or vegetable fat which contains very little water and produces pastry with crisp "short" texture.

SOUR CREAM: Cream soured by lactic acid used for sauces and salad dressings.

SPUN SUGAR: Sugar boiled to caramel stage, 380°F, cooled slightly and drawn into thin threads for decorating desserts and cakes.

STEAMER: Double saucepan with lower part for water and upper container perforated to allow steam through to cook food.

STEAM BAKE: To cook food in a bain-marie in the oven so that it remains moist during slow cooking.

SYRUP: Sugar and water boiled together.

TAPIOCA: Starch granules made from the cassava plant which become transparent and gelatinous when cooked.

TEFLON: Non-stick finish to cooking utensils.

TORTE: (German) Continental cake with ground nuts and breadcrumbs and little or no flour.

TREACLE: (Molasses) Dark viscous by-product of sugar refining.

VANILLA BEAN: Seed pod of the vanilla orchid, dried and used for flavoring by infusing in milk or stored in a jar of sugar to make vanilla sugar. Pod should be split as seeds are particularly aromatic.

VERMICELLI: (Italian) Pasta drawn into thin threads finer than spaghetti.

YEAST: A living organism that acts as a leavening agent for dough. There are two types available: active dry yeast and compressed fresh yeast. The former is less perishable.

ZEST: Fine outer rind of citrus fruits which contains aromatic oil. Removed in thin slivers, avoiding pith, for infusing, or finely grated for flavoring or garnish.

Index